in the Librar

Bibliography in the Bookshop

Bibliography in the Bookshop

F. Seymour Smith

**Second edition entirely
revised and rewritten**

 ANDRE DEUTSCH / A Grafton Book

First published 1964 by
André Deutsch Limited
105 Great Russell Street London WC1

Copyright © 1964, 1972 by F. Seymour Smith
Second edition 1972
All rights reserved

Printed in Great Britain by
Ebenezer Baylis and Son Ltd
The Trinity Press, Worcester, and London

ISBN 0 233 95971 8

Contents

Preface to the Second Edition

When *Bibliography in the Bookshop* was published in 1964, some long-delayed changes and developments in the British book trade were at last being seriously discussed. No clearer proof of progress made since then need be offered now than the simple statement that by 1970, when a new edition was necessary, mere revision of the book was found to be unsatisfactory, and quite inadequate for the needs of bookseller students of a new generation.

Hence, for this new edition, more than half the text has been completely rewritten, new material added, outdated comments and information deleted, and the whole radically revised.

The new syllabus for the BA Diploma in Bookselling retains *Bookshop Bibliography*, with the addition of a separate section called *Bibliography and Classification*, taking the place of a former section *Applied Bibliography*. A new section for which students are required to study, *Books and the Mind of Man*, is strongly influenced, and was almost brought into being, by the great IPEX Exhibition in London of 1963. This section deals with creative literature of Great Britain, Europe and America through the centuries from the incunabula of the fifteenth century to Churchill.

Bibliography in the Bookshop, in some ways complementary to my *An English Library*, is not only for students receiving personal tuition, but is especially intended to help Commonwealth booksellers and others who may not have any chance of attending lectures, college seminars or other courses of instruction organized by the Booksellers Association.

Correspondence courses in bookselling offered by Wolsey Hall have long been established. In 1968, in cooperation with the BA, an entirely new course was prepared, based on the new syllabus. This textbook should be of particular use to those taking the Wolsey Hall course.

For such students, I have added at the end of chapters two

to twelve in parts one and two, some key questions emphasizing the most important topics for candidates sitting examinations. Most of the specific bibliographies and standard books cited have been priced, but merely for guidance, to enable students to learn the price categories of the books they may have to mention in answers. Prices continue to rise annually, and all entries should therefore be checked from time to time with publishers' latest catalogues.

My thanks are due to booksellers for criticisms and suggestions arising from the 1964 edition, and I wish to thank Mr F. Davids Thomsen, Managing Director of the Almqvist and Wiksell Group of Booksellers, Stockholm, for his interest in the book, and for his kind permission to reprint in appendix one, his detailed description in English, of the truly remarkable and exemplary *Bibliography in Action* service offered by his group in Sweden and other countries of northern Europe.

Bexhill, Sussex   F. SEYMOUR SMITH
                                                               May, 1971

Part One
The Service of a Charter Bookseller

Chapter 1
'A Staff Skilled in Bibliography'

It was in the early 1930's, when radio talks were beginning to be accepted as a new method of popular education, that G. K. Chesterton dryly observed we had invented broadcasting just at the time when we had nothing important to say.

This genial witticism came to my mind when a colleague said that *Bibliography in the Bookshop* had been published just at the time when the subject was on the way out in Britain in all but a few great bookshops. Is this true of the 1970's? Certainly the 1960's was a trying, testing decade. Those who may gloomily agree with the statement are able to produce evidence of some decline in the standard of book service offered to the public.

Yet, never before has the book trade in Britain provided such a comprehensive and imaginative training syllabus as the current one. Never before has the Booksellers Association given so much money, time and effort, under the direction of experienced specialists, to education and training for better bookselling in Great Britain.

Indeed, by the time DITB (Distributive Industries Training Board) became fully effective, with a compulsory levy for the establishment of training facilities in wholesaling and retailing, the BA had already developed ideas and schemes which had been under discussion since 1947.

We still lack the ideal of a full-time Institute of Bookselling, with a residential college, but the Manchester and the Brighton Schools of Bookselling are in full swing, and there are other examples of a new endeavour to bring our bookselling service up to the best now offered in Scandinavian, German and some other European bookshops.

Nor should we overlook the comprehensive and varied training facilities established in London, not only officially by the BA, but also by W. H. Smith and Son, whose work in this field in regional centres has for long been widely praised. With its great resources and its traditional recognition of the importance of staff training and education, dating back to the Victorian era when such ideas were uncommon in commerce, this multiple firm of book wholesalers and retailers established in 1971 at Milton Hill House, near Didcot in Berkshire, a Staff Training College to take the place of regional training centres formerly provided in London and Birmingham.

In all schemes of training bookshop bibliography has an important place. It must never be allowed to be depreciated. Where it is absolutely necessary to provide a bibliographical service, as in university and technical bookshops, in library booksellers' distribution centres, and above all in export bookselling firms, the demand from specialized customers increases both in quantity and quality. In smaller, general bookshops, and shops where the sale of books is only a part of the total trading, staff and customers will see to it that a bibliographical service is not neglected. Staff because of pride in their work and of knowledge (as well as personal interest) acquired whilst in training; customers because they will continue to insist on booksellers fulfilling their function as retailers of a very specialized type, recognized in all civilized countries as essential to the full development of the community in an era of the Open University, television and radio public education, and intensive national educational facilities from primary school to colleges of further education and full-time university studies.

'A stockholding bookseller may also carry on some ancillary or associated business in conjunction with his business of selling books, such as the sale of stationery or of certain kinds of fancy goods, but his principal business is that of a bookseller holding a varied stock of books, employing a staff skilled in bibliography and offering to a greater or less degree all the services associated with the business of a first-rate bookseller.'

This long, but singularly apt quotation is taken from the judgment of the Restrictive Practices Court, read on Tuesday, 30th October 1962, by Mr Justice Buckley. Readers of this book will note with special interest the final clauses of the passage, and will, it is hoped, have read the full report in the *Bookseller* (3rd November 1962, pages 1824–1858). Later on in this book the temptation to quote from it again will not be resisted. But for the time being, it will be convenient to emphasize the importance placed by the Court on the essential need for a first-rate bookseller to employ 'a staff skilled in bibliography'.

No good bookseller would question this view; no book-buying member of the public would disagree. Everybody concerned must endorse it, and welcome Mr Justice Buckley's reference to bibliography in the bookshop in this historic judgment, which deserves to be read in full by every entrant into the trade.

Booksellers are proud of this public recognition of those special aspects of their work requiring special skills and knowledge, which are indeed the subject of this textbook.

Supermarkets and book merchandising techniques are not to be viewed scornfully even by dedicated bookmen on both sides of the cash desk. Traders benefit financially with the result that they are the better able to afford the cost of staff training and the employment of qualified assistants. Customers with specialized book needs are attracted to such general bookshops and if their orders for books not stocked are filled reasonably well, are satisfied.

'Everybody uses the supermarket' replied a distinguished bookseller under cross-examination in the 'trial' of the NBA. This remark brought welcome laughter into the courtroom. It also deepened understanding of the position of a charter bookseller in a non-academic town. There was common ground of agreement between both sides; it was agreed that the service of a good bookshop to the community could never be offered by supermarketeering and merchandising. Students who are interested should read the full report of and commentary on this historic case.[1]

What then, are these special services required by book-buyers? Why is it necessary that in this era of self-service and cut-price retailing they should be made available 'to a greater or less degree'? And where should booksellers draw the line which decides how far they can go in degree in their varying types of bookselling? Finally, is it practicable to try to establish a minimum standard of service? Answers to these fundamental questions will be suggested as this study proceeds.

The first question is the simplest to answer because it is merely necessary to list representative routine enquiries and orders that may be selected from any large bookselling firm's daily post. Here then, are a few selected as fair examples from the work of one bibliographical office where the intake of

1. *Books Are Different: an account of the defence of the NBA*, edited by R. E. Barker and G. R. Davies. Macmillan, 1966, pp. 284 *et seq.*

serious enquiries requiring bibliographical knowledge and a trained staff reached in the 1960's an average annual total of about 1,200, plus another thousand requests for subject book-lists. They came from every section of the community: bookstall and shop customers, branch book assistants, public and university libraries, technical and industrial libraries, scientific libraries and service libraries, institutional and academic libraries, wholesalers and retailers at home and abroad.

This is a random selection, providing a practical background to this course of instruction in bookshop bibliography.

a. *We require a buying list on world history: standard books, both American and British; a few popular books and a few school text-books up to GCE 'A' Level.*

b. *Our school library has been allocated £500 for basic stock purchases. Recreational books only, not class books. Please advise us about suitable books in all classes, including fiction. Reading age groups from about 10 to 16.*

c. *We are sending you a customer's catalogue of his private library in India. He is giving this library away to needy scholars and students, and wishes us to suggest volumes to replace it in its entirety, as he has read or used everything in the existing collection. The catalogue is classified by Dewey Decimal Classification which his secretary-librarian has applied to this library. Please send your suggestions for up to about £1,000's worth of books in English, classified by the same scheme, thus ensuring complete coverage of our client's interests, but avoiding duplication of titles already read.*

d. *Please send a copy of the best and most scholarly edition of 'Gulliver's Travels' now in print, price immaterial; together with a bibliography of all Swift's works in print and some standard books of biography and criticism relating to this author.*

e. *We want about a dozen authoritative monographs and critical works by the foremost English writers on poets of the Romantic Period in English Literature.*

f. *Send a booklist of available material on the teaching of Mathematics and History in English schools, all grades.*

g. *What parallel text editions are there of Greek and Latin Classics? Are there any French-English parallel texts?*

h. *Have you any textbooks for university students in stock on the following subjects: Limnology; Conchology, . . . If not, send a list of suggested titles.*

i. We are interested in Costume; Puppetry; Art Books, reproducing Flower Paintings, Roses, etc. What is there to buy? Upper price limit about three pounds.

j. A bookstall manager: 'One of my customers for newspapers and magazines collects tableglass. He asks, "Have you any information you can send him through me on books that might interest and help? Price no object." '

k. Will you recommend some good historical novels dealing with the following periods? . . .

l. We can sell all biographies and autobiographies, and even good fiction, about doctors and medical life, actors, and lawyers. Please recommend as many as you can, hardcover and paperback editions.

m. Will you recommend and supply on approval three or four authoritative books on problems arising from social class and status, contemporary social psychology in Britain, and allied themes.

n. We want a number of books on architecture in England from Roman occupation to 1900, considered as a part of social history (that is, on domestic architecture, peasants' and other cottages, churches, town houses, country villas, manor houses).

o. What is the best reference book on idiomatic and proverbial phrases, with origins and anecdotes?

p. Please list and supply all available books by all prize-winning authors: English, American, and anything translated into English.

One could go on, for such enquiries are never-ceasing and as varied as books and authors. My selection is from actual daily work in the only trade bibliographical office in which I have had personal experience. Many readers of this book will be able to add to the list, but my purpose here is to show entrants into the book trade and student booksellers a little of what bookshop bibliography means in daily practice.[2]

The bookseller has to consider whether his shop and staff can tackle such enquiries, and then he must decide if it will be profitable to undertake this work. Here, much depends on the type of his business; the quality and quantity of his staffing; the bibliographical equipment he is able to provide and the extramural resources he can call upon without wasting time.

As one customer exclaimed when he made an even more comprehensive request for assistance than anything quoted above: 'Well, it's a tall order.' It is unnecessary to discuss

2. See also *Books Are Different*, pp. 300–304.

further the importance of this service, for those who make this type of enquiry are people who want to buy books; have the money to pay for what they require, and show their goodwill by asking for information and advice.

Individual booksellers have to decide where they have to draw the line between service and refusal, but certainly the minimum standard required of a charter bookseller should at least be offered. Staff engaged on this bibliographical service must be trained to bring to the surface information buried in trade and other bibliographical sources, and their book world is infinite because of the hundreds of thousands of books in print – millions if we include foreign publications.

The purpose of the search is to bring the right book to the customer as quickly and economically as possible under varying circumstances, which indeed extend from the simplest enquiries to the inspiring and exemplary service described in Appendix 1.

Students working in smaller bookshops, perhaps in stores where books are only one section of the business, the remainder being concerned with 'the sale of stationery or of certain kinds of fancy goods', will realize that some enquiries they will receive must be outside the scope of their own daily work, but they should not be outside their sphere of interest. In many instances these assistants will later work in larger shops, or may even seek bookshop appointments in Europe or America.

Even the largest bookshops in Britain with the greatest stock, will of course have on the shelves and in warehouse book stock, only a small fraction of the books in print at any given period. Because of this, paradoxically, it is rather more important and useful to know something about books not in stock.

Customers are well served if assistants can locate quickly any stock title required, flicking the volume deftly off the shelf in a trice. This is a trick of the trade and the sign of the well-trained assistant.

But there are many books demanding some knowledge of their contents and quality, and a good deal of experienced salesmanship, to ensure that they will reach the public they were written for, and the customers who will readily buy them if expert publicity is used by the local bookseller as well as the publisher.

Bookselling at this level requires more than training and a good memory, but fortunately the very nature of the work creates enthusiasm of the sort that has made many bookshops legendary. When developing a flair or instinct for good books and likely customers, many assistants will rightly seek to achieve some degree of specialization. That is, they will acquire a knowledge of specific classes of books far beyond the superficial. Nor will they allow this personal study to be limited by their own stock.

The building up of a home collection of books reflecting the taste and interests of the bookseller is a sure sign of a born bookman. Therefore one would recommend all students to select a few subjects and authors and to master the literature connected with them. Their choice will of course reflect their own development over a period of years and even if certain branches of knowledge cease to interest them eventually, what they have acquired will always be at the service of others.

Moreover, there is no better method than this of preparing for examination questions in which candidates are expected to offer lists of books on nominated subjects and authors with precise bibliographical details. Such questions are sometimes linked to tests on a general knowledge of the basic stock of a bookshop. Some attention will be given to this subject later, but the importance of some specialization at the start of a bookshop career will be clearly understood by all students. This sort of knowledge cannot be acquired quickly, but it begins to lodge in the mind from one's first few weeks in a bookshop or a library; it is added to continually without much effort, little by little, day after day, throughout one's working life. This continual mental activity is an essential part of bookmanship, for the information about books and authors is retained over the years, waiting like water from a deep well to be drawn to the surface when required.

John Wilson of the once famous firm of Edward Bumpus of Oxford Street in London, gathered an encyclopaedic knowledge of books and authors during his long lifetime of bookselling. When he died there was scarcely another, one could name to take his place in the trade. After a visit to his shop and half an hour's book gossip I often reflected that Sydney Smith's witty remark about Lord Macaulay could well be applied to him: 'He not only overflowed with learning, but stood in the slop.'

Chapter 2
Bibliography: its Meanings and History

It is now necessary for us to consider exactly what we mean by the term bibliography, which has been used so frequently in the opening chapter, particularly in its application to the daily work of a bookseller.

The *Oxford English Dictionary* gives us the derivation and history of the word, dating changes in use and meaning through the centuries from 1678. Then bibliography meant the writing, that is the copying, of manuscripts and books: thus, in the seventeenth century a bibliographer was a scribe who copied. Not until 1814 did a secondary meaning appear: then bibliography meant the systematic description of books: authorship, printing, publication, editions. From this use we derive the application of 'a bibliography' to a list or book containing these details, often limited to specific subjects and authors.

By 1869 we find it used as it is today: meaning 'a list of the books of a particular author, printer, country: the literature of a subject'.

It is this last precise meaning that chiefly concerns us here, because it is the subject of the diploma examinations in bibliography and classification. Just over a century old, the term so-defined in OED is the consequence of interest in book-collecting, authorship, private and public libraries, and first or early editions, encouraged by the former aspect of bibliography as defined in 1814.

For booksellers, this is the background of their bookshop bibliographical service. Subdivisions to be considered are Trade Bibliography, Author Bibliography, Subject Bibliography. Each division requires a technique to be mastered and used as a tool by those who are asked to compile buying lists, to search for accurate information about published material in book form, to answer questions about books in print.

The bookshop bibliographer must on occasion trace and record details of authorship, editions, scope, contents, and grade of the selected literature of a specified subject available from time to time. He may also be expected to evaluate chosen books on subjects and authors of his special spheres of book knowledge.

If his work is that of an antiquarian bookseller he will need to pursue this fascinating topic even further, for the demands of book collectors are usually more specialized and erudite than those of the average customer. Dealers in first editions, second-hand, out of print, and perhaps scarce books will be required to extend their studies to what is now called 'historical bibliography'.

A textbook on this topic deals with manuscripts, handwriting, papermaking, block books, the invention of movable type, the history of printing from that period to the present, bookbinding, private presses, typography, woodcuts, engraving, book illustration, publishing, bookselling and copyright. That is, briefly, with the complete history of the Book.

This is not our subject. Nor is descriptive bibliography, as defined by R. B. McKerrow, author of a classic work *An Introduction to Bibliography for Literary Students*. McKerrow's work at the British Museum, and his book, clarified thought and practice in the whole field of historical bibliography, especially when applied to the detailed examination of specific texts, and to literary history generally.

From his studies and method, textual editors have learned a great deal, deriving from McKerrow the new term 'descriptive bibliography'. By classification, not chance, *Introduction to Bibliography for Literary Students* is the first book entered in the great *Oxford General Catalogue*. Nothing could be more apt, for behind the scholarship of so many standard editions in this catalogue are textual studies exemplifying the soundness of his teaching.

Descriptive bibliography in this century has been concerned with the examination of specific books for the purpose of settling problems of doubtful or unknown authorship; with verification of details connected with first or early editions, chronology, dating, imprints, paper, and allied matters, including the establishment or rejection of textual variations.

The value of this science to editors of standard texts and to literary historians is clear. To cite two authors as examples I will select Daniel Defoe and Jonathan Swift. Definitive texts, and problems of authorship which have arisen from the study of these two prolific writers could scarcely have proceeded as they have done without descriptive bibliographical techniques.

One may note, too, the importance of the work done by scholars in the establishment of definitive texts of Henry Vaughan, Thomas Traherne and John Donne. The subject has often the interest of detective work, especially when we read of the tests made to decide if a first edition should be accepted or whether it is doubtful. Pirated, imitated and forged editions have been exposed by methodical application of the principles of descriptive bibliography, but we cannot dwell upon it here, because it is an academic, not a trade subject, except for antiquarian booksellers and book collectors.

When touching upon this, I cited McKerrow's *Introduction to Bibliography*. By coincidence the next book in the *Oxford General Catalogue* provides a perfect example of McKerrow's method: a textbook by the doyen of American bibliographical editors, Fredson Bowers, whose *Bibliography and Textual Criticism* (1964) explains and discusses his theory and practice. His edition of the *Dramatic Works* of Thomas Dekker, four volumes, *CUP*, is not likely ever to be superseded.

A final example is worth noting: I have before me a seasonal brochure from OUP for July 1970, in which a revision of an essay on *Shakespeare and the New Bibliography* by F. P. Wilson, edited by Helen Gardner, was announced with a note recalling achievements of the school of Pollard, McKerrow, and Greg to remind us of the three great names in this branch of bibliography.

Bookshop bibliography is a practical everyday method of searching for the information required before certain orders can be filled by the bookseller and the detailed lists asked for by customers, especially institutional, technical and export customers, can be prepared.

If students will now turn again to Appendix 1 they will understand from the description of the Almqvist and Wiksell Bokhandel Documentation Centre at Stockholm, how this service is organized and for what purpose, in a country where the book trade is virtually international. 'Research does not know of any boundary lines' writes Mr F. Davids Thomsen. His group's *List of Subjects* is systematically arranged by a scheme of classification covering all of classes 500 and 600 in Dewey's

Classification, with many subjects from class 300, 700 and 900. It would seem that this Swedish service has developed to an ideal standard and may be unique in Europe.

In the next chapter I will therefore describe the various bibliographies and sources of bibliographical information that are the tools of the British bookseller's trade enabling him to offer a similar service varied in degree according to his type of trade and his resources.

Some of these sources are essential and are rightly obligatory for all stockholding charter booksellers; the others will usually be available only in larger bookshops and in those with academic and institutional trade.

Every bibliography and source named should be thoroughly known by every diploma student, whether he is likely to use the full sequence or only a section. Customers are sometimes unreasonable, and their demands are often made in ignorance of the realities of business life and limitations of today.

It is therefore necessary for assistants to learn how to deal with troublesome customers, politely but firmly. One would not hesitate to recommend them to go to a public library for advice and information if that seemed the best source at which to make the type of enquiries demanding research before the placing of an order.

One example may be cited: a customer asked for a list of a dozen contemporary novels before giving a firm order, stipulating that each title listed must be annotated with a précis of the plot in which special attention should be given to any religious discussion and sectarian bias. Current publications in stock did not interest him. This request having been made by letter it was a matter of office routine to send a written suggestion, which concluded with the address of his nearest public library. Nothing more was heard from him.

Library authorities agree that it is one of the functions of a modern reference library service to provide an extra-mural source of information to local tradesmen, especially to local booksellers, and although even a modern reference librarian would probably consider such a request beyond the limit, he would almost certainly have placed at the disposal of the enquirer a few suitable bibliographies, such as *British Book News* and a file of the *Times Literary Supplement* from which he could make his own selection.

Care should be taken, however, not to discourage potential bookbuyers whose knowledge of what they really require may be vague due to inability to state precisely their needs, and to ignorance of bookshops and current publications. Entrants to the trade will as a matter of course refer proposed rejections to a senior.

QUESTIONS FOR RECAPITULATION

1. Define the term bibliography, illustrating in your answer changes in meaning from the seventeenth century to the present time, and indicating the various types of bibliography now in use.

2. Describe the work of a bookshop bibliographer serving academic, scientific and technical customers, public libraries and specialist customers.

3. What is the A.W. Documentation Centre and how does it function?

Chapter 3
The Tools of the Book Trade: 1

Trade bibliography of necessity is largely concerned with customers' orders for books not normally stocked, and with an extension of service in order to promote sales of specific books. Daily use of the tools of the trade should result in knowledge of current and back-list publications which may affect stock. How do we know certain books of the past exist at all and are available until we search for them? When the information is tracked down we do not always limit this newly acquired knowledge to the single customer making the initiating enquiry.

Complicated problems of the contemporary trade are still largely unsolved when they are concerned with quick and efficient distribution, and with the prompt filling of single copy orders for customers who cannot choose from stock. Stock-holding booksellers vary from those able to carry a thousand volumes, through medium-size firms with about 8,000 volumes, to the great 'aristocrat' class (Mr Justice Buckley's category) offering their customers a choice from 20,000 volumes to the plenitude of Blackwell's of Oxford, where more than 100,000 'titles' are carried, 'many of which are stocked in quantity'.[1]

Customers' orders may bring no profit worth accounting for to the smaller bookshop; may even mean providing this service at a slight loss. Much depends on terms for singles, and on the price of the books so supplied.

The bookbuying public and journalists outside the trade press find this hard to believe, their scepticism providing the sort of publicity certain to crop up perennially in the popular press, magazines and radio journalism. Reluctance, and nowadays, refusal, to accept a certain type of customers' orders arouses anger in publishers and their authors, as well as despair in frustrated buyers. In one firm acceptable orders are restricted to books published by a selected list of publishers, numbering it is true, about four hundred, but still excluding

1. See *Books Are Different*, p. 9.

scores of others whose specialized publications are often of importance for technical and scientific reasons.

We are still not in the 'shelf-service only' era in Britain, but seem to be drawing nearer to it than when the first edition of this book was published. Dedicated bookmen, warmly commended in the 1962 Judgment which showed acute understanding of their problems in an age of increasing economic troubles, are rarer, and their survival depends on the support they receive and deserve from the towns they serve, their local libraries and educational libraries, their regional customers spending money on books for great commercial enterprises, colleges of commerce and technology.

On such sources of trade as these depends the economic justification of the bookseller for providing the expensive, necessary tools of his trade. The dilemma is obvious: in order to attract this profitable type of business, the bookseller must offer the service; but in order to be able financially to provide the service he must be sure of attracting the business.

However small the service, there are a few tools which all will agree are the minimum. Foremost in British bookshops, the trade bibliographical services of the old-established firm of J. Whitaker and Sons enable even the smallest shop to function reasonably well. Whitaker crops up many times in most examination papers and answers, but years of experience have convinced me that a percentage of students will always spell the name with two t's; even more students will frequently refer to 'Whittaker's Cumulative Book Index' instead of Whitaker's *Cumulative Book List*.

Slapdash attention to everyday details loses marks, and all too often occurs in 'borderline candidates', serving to push the candidate over the border – on the wrong side. It is worth while paying careful attention to these minutiae.

Another tip: make sure that you remember the complete contents and function of every trade book you handle in your daily work, and of as many standard reference books as you stock or handle. These two points will be enlarged upon specifically as we proceed with this course of study, because meticulous attention to details is one mark of the well-trained bibliographer.

The names of authors and the titles of their books (and of publishers) will of course frequently be quoted, written, typed:

therefore leave such annoying errors as Middleton Murray, J. B. Priestly, *Allan Quartermain*, George Elliott, John Keat's, Edgar Alan Poe, Noel Streatfield, Harold Nicholson, Weidenfield and Nicholsen, Cassel, Bless, Collin's, Chamber's . . . and so on, to the ignorant or slipshod. See to it right at the beginning of your career in bookselling that you get these things correct: Middleton Murry, J. B. Priestley, *Allan Quatermain*, George Eliot, John Keats's, Edgar Allan Poe, Noel Streatfeild, Harold Nicolson . . . and of course Hans Andersen and Jane Austen.

This small list of examples may cause some students to smile, but every one has come my way, and the need for care is therefore evident, before we turn our attention to the specific trade bibliographies of an agreed minimum service. So we will first of all take from our bookshop reference collection of trade bibliographies:

British Books in Print: the Reference Catalogue of Current Literature, published by J. Whitaker and Sons. Since 1965 this self-explanatory index has been published annually, usually in October in two fat quarto volumes. The 1971 edition totals 4,500 pages, and has entries for 240,000 books available up to April, 1971.

I have said above, 'this self-explanatory index'; but even with this work, it is necessary to make quite certain what it offers the user. Hence: examine the contents carefully, noting the supplementary information it contains in the 'prelims', as befits 'the bookseller's bible'. Read the preface with as much attention as the clergy are said to read the annual preface to their *Crockford's Directory* – although for different reasons.

The history behind *British Books in Print: 1971* will interest every bookseller. It started with what is now its subtitle, namely, as the *Reference Catalogue of Current Literature* published at varying intervals, sometimes every two years, later every four years. One would suppose that the first edition of 1874 would be an interesting item in an antiquarian catalogue. At that time, almost one hundred years ago, and up to 1932, the *Reference Catalogue* comprised publishers' catalogues (only 135 in 1874) bound together in uniform size, in two thick volumes, with a third providing an index of authors and titles in one A–Z sequence, later altered to two separate sequences. I have the index volume for 1906 near my office desk, strongly bound in heavy legal buckram, gilt edged, 916 pages.

The complete set of catalogues and index was a mighty work to handle and to house: about two feet of shelf space being required in those spacious days, because by 1932 the catalogues alone occupied four great volumes.

By 1936 the *Reference Catalogue* had assumed its familiar format in two large quartos, providing the searcher with details of books from 652 publishing firms, and appearing at two-yearly intervals. By 1961 the 135 publishers of 1874 had increased to 1,843: the 35,000 index entries had grown to 350,000 in two volumes of 2,744 pages. By 1969 the publishers numbered 3,500, and a new detail had been added, Standard Book Numbers for the latest publications; later annual issues will give complete SBN. Thus in a hundred years this world-famous tool of the British book trade has progressed from minor clerical editing of a small group of publishers' catalogues to a huge, computerized index for the use of everybody concerned with tracing and ordering books, from the modestly staffed private bookseller to the greatest, computerized library and institutional buyer in the world of books.

There were a number of important changes in the October 1971 edition, published at £15 net. Completely 'computer-generated', the entries were submitted to the various publishers as 'print-outs' of their lists, thus making it possible for a final check to be made before the index was passed for press. This procedure will substantially decrease chances of error. The greatest change was the reversion to one a–z alphabetical sequence of authors and titles, authors' names being printed in bold type.

In such a huge undertaking as the current *British Books in Print* perfection is impossible: the coverage is bound to be incomplete. Time was when a complete publisher's list would be omitted (probably because the publisher's staff omitted to send in details), but nowadays one seldom finds *lacunae*. It helps if errors and omissions, when found, are noted. Whitaker's editor invites such reports. But when using *British Books in Print* remember that this index is not a record of new and annual publications; it is exactly what the title implies: a record 'of books in print and on sale in the United Kingdom' at the time of final compilation, which is about six months before the month of November of each year. If this minor point appears to be laboured, it is because a minority of students are unable to express clearly the difference between *British Books in Print* and the next standard reference tool of the trade, namely *Whitaker's Cumulative Book List*, which is indeed a record of the fact of publication, whether the books listed therein are in print and available on sale or are not. Hence, you will search in vain for an entry for a book entitled *British Books in Print* in the book bearing that title. This is not the result of careless omission but merely because by the time of going to press of each annual volume, the preceding volume is out of print. But you will find an entry for the book in the annual volume of the *Cumulative Book List*, or CBL as we will call it. This is a trade bibliography which cannot be superseded, whereas the yearly publication of the former work really renders the preceding volume obsolete. We discard it every December; CBL we keep, year after year until lack of filing space compels us to discard early volumes.

As a record of permanent usefulness, CBL is a cumulation of entries, starting with the weekly lists in the *Bookseller* which are cumulated in *Books of the Month* (see page 28); then again cumulated quarterly, each quarter superseding the last one up to Jan.–Sept., which itself is superseded by the annual volume, Jan.–Dec.

Publication of this annual cumulation in a cloth, hardcover reference quarto, completes an indispensable service to subscribers, except for the five-year cumulations, which started with the 1948–1952 volume. Obviously the search for an entry is shortened if one is able to cut out reference to five separate volumes. There is a minor point to notice: annual volumes of CBL retain the entry of new publications under 47 conventional trade classifications, or groups in part one, together with a Fiction section divided into eight categories according to the predominant types of current novels; part two provides the usual A–Z author/title sequence. In the five-year cumulations, however, part one of each volume has been discarded, and the fat quarto reference work is now in one A–Z sequence. Daily usage of the latest five-year index, for the period 1963–1967, should make these details clear, helping the well-trained assistant to search speedily and with precision instead of in the awkward, time-wasting method of those who fumble backwards and forwards in ignorance.

I have referred to *Books of the Month* as the stage in the

compilation of CBL which leads to the quarterly instalments. Now we should learn a little more about this recent addition to the Whitaker book service. Not only does this monthly index list the books published in the past month, but it also records the publication of forthcoming books for the next two months, all in one alphabetical sequence. Forthcoming books are starred in the left margin, with month of proposed publication given in parentheses – precise date if notified by the publisher. Hence the full title of the index, which started in January 1970, is Whitaker's *Books of the Month and Books to Come*, the annual subscription (in 1972) being £7.20

We should not overlook another, well-established and famous trade bibliography, known all over the world as the *English Catalogue of Books*, with an ancestry even older than its rival, for the *English Catalogue* was formerly the *London Catalogue*; and later the *British Catalogue*, going back to 1773. The *English Catalogue of Books* was first so-called in 1835, and was formerly cumulated from weekly lists in the old *Publishers Circular and Booksellers Record* (1837).

It is now cumulated from monthly supplements to *The Publisher*, the journal of the publishing industry. Each supplement consists of an author index, a separate title index, with separate sequences for paperbacks; and for maps and atlases. Books published in both hardcover and paperback editions are asterisked. Cataloguing is of a high standard, with exact dates of publication where supplied by publishers. Thus, *Books of the Month Supplement* has notable and useful features. The Publishers Circular Ltd., also issue eight special supplements every year: four seasonal, one paperbacks, one junior books, one religious books, and one devoted to technical books.

Librarians will be interested to learn that the reprint firm of Kraus of New York, in cooperation with The Publishers Circular Ltd., have issued reprints of early volumes and cumulations, from 1801 to 1951, the complete set costing £555.

Examples of trade bibliographies discussed so far I regard as the minimum with which even the smallest bookshop should be equipped if a reasonable service is to be offered to customers requiring more than a stock choice. In the next chapter details will be given of a secondary group, still of very great importance, but not usually available to the staff of smaller firms.

QUESTIONS FOR RECAPITULATION

1. Describe *British Books in Print* in detail, concluding with a brief history of this standard trade bibliography.

2. What is *Whitaker's Cumulative Book List*? In your answer be careful to give precise details of its use to the book trade and to librarians, and indicate how it is compiled.

3. What is the *English Catalogue of Books*? Do you think this trade bibliography should be provided for staff use in bookshops where *British Books in Print* is stocked for reference?

Chapter 4
The Tools of the Book Trade: 2

Every British book trade bibliography has its counterpart in the USA. Indeed during the last fifty years I think it will be agreed generally that American bibliographers have set a standard for others in the world of books.

The American equivalent of Whitaker's service comes to us principally from the famous firm of R. R. Bowker Company, now a Xerox Company whose editorial and subscription offices are in New York; and the H. W. Wilson Company of Chicago and New York.

Books in Print is a well-established model for *British Books in Print*. Published annually (usually available late October) these two handsome quarto volumes list by author and title about 310,000 books from 1,900 US publishers (1970 estimates). The title index volume provides names and addresses of all known US publishers, with eventually ISBN (international Standard Book Numbers), and the set costs $30·25 outside North America. Only larger bookshops are able to provide this admirable tool for staff. However, an increasing number of local public and other libraries subscribe, and thus may be willing to offer an extra-mural service to local shops.

The basis of *Books in Print* is a vast compilation, rather like the former *Reference Catalogue* described in the previous chapter, called *Publishers' Trade List Annual*. By 1970 this set of trade order lists of the 1,900 US publishers, had grown to six quarto volumes.

The Bowker service is now further enhanced in usefulness by a two-volumed annual *Subject Guide to Books in Print*, published in October as a complete subject listing of all the books entered in the current *Publishers' Trade List Annual*. Nothing comparable is done for *British Books in Print*. Its value for larger bookshops need not be stressed: others should be able to consult it in public libraries; certain types of customer, such as commercial and technical librarians, will use it extensively for compiling orders for standard American books of a specialized nature.

Here we now turn to the American equivalent of our *Bookseller*: the lively, informative *Publishers' Weekly*, well sub-titled the *Book Industry Journal*. Every issue is packed with articles, advertisements and advance information. All the important books eventually find British or British-American publishers. Hence, every bookshop should subscribe to this trade magazine, even if only to decide what to reject or to be wary of. From its pages the bookseller with a flair and vast experience will estimate 'flops', 'naturals', 'probables', 'doubt-fuls'. He will be in the know regarding bestsellers and important publications long before they reach Britain, and in these days of near-commuting between New York and London by a certain restless, eager type of businessman, such knowledge comes in useful when answering customers' enquiries.

To give only one example: a telephoned enquiry about a new (and perhaps rather sensational) book on the advertising 'racket' could give an assistant a great deal of trouble in a fruitless search for something that the customer is certain has been published. But a bookshop subscribing to *Publishers' Weekly* will provide all staff with the knowledge that the book in question is published, but as yet, only in New York, where it has created a storm of discussion likely to bring the book to London within a few months.

There are other features worth attention. The 'Weekly Record' (I like the precise terminology) of new books is virtually perfect, being based entirely on the cataloguing of the experts and specialists in Library of Congress, with the addition of the published prices, and even, when necessary, the addresses of publishers. Moreover, every entry is classified by the Dewey Decimal Classification, thus revealing at a glance (at least to librarians and booksellers familiar with the system) the precise subject of non-fiction books; most authors have dates of birth, etc., given; brief annotations are provided indicating the contents and range of certain classes of publica-tion, prepared 'so far as possible from actual examination of the finished books' – this is very important.

It is doubtful if trade bibliography can or need go beyond this exemplary standard, maintained consistently, and unique in the world of books, for there are many other useful features, such as the indication of certain popular types of 'brand' fiction for guidance of the 'pop' shops; the probable markets for non-fiction books; changes of title for some reprints; topic and category indications for most novels. This last is indicated by conventional, easily remembered abbreviations: FIC-S informs, perhaps warns, us that the novels so captioned are 'Science' fiction fantasies (Sf); FIC-W = Westerns; FIC-M = Crime fiction; and JUV = junior fiction (non-fiction for young readers is designated by 'j' prefixed to the classification number). Volumes of short stories such as Noël Coward's *Bon Voyage* receive detailed listing of contents by title. American book-sellers and librarians have never 'asked for more' from their 'Weekly Record'; but one imagines that if they were to, their requests would be agreed to at once.

In fact, R. R. Bowker Company forestalled requests for a subject catalogue of their weekly author listing, by producing in the 1960's a truly remarkable *American Book Publishing Record* (BPR) published monthly. Entries are as catalogued by Library of Congress, annotated by the staff of *Publishers' Weekly*, and are arranged in Dewey Decimal Classification order, with author and title indexes. Such a monthly cumulation is of permanent value, with its separate sections for children's books, fiction, and even talking books (i.e. phonorecords). Well-printed, and often running to nearly 150 pages of double-printed entries, BPR is to American book publishing what our next standard bibliography is to British

The reference here is to *The British National Bibliography* (BNB). BNB, now well-established and widely used and respected all over the world, is one of two bibliographical services on the grand scale, serving the book trade, but both designed to offer scholars and indeed the whole world of books in English com-plete, professionally compiled records of greater scope and wider function than any work hitherto described. Students must for examination purposes, if not for their daily work, have a detailed, practical knowledge of BNB.

As its title implies it is a national bibliography; but note that a national bibliography may be of two different types. One: it may be a record of everything published, not only in, but about, a specific country. As such, it should record books in all languages, wherever they may be published. The sole qualifica-

tion for inclusion is that all books must relate to the
country concerned: historical monographs, descriptive works,
fiction, and so on. A famous example of this type of national
bibliography may be cited in any question on the subject:
Mendelssohn's *South African Bibliography*, 2 volumes, Kegan
Paul, 1910; reprinted in a limited facsimile edition, Arco, 1957,
2, 256pp., quarto. This is a *catalogue raisonné* of a great collection
of books relating to South Africa. For yet another colossal
bibliographical undertaking in this field remember Sir John
Alexander Ferguson's *Bibliography of Australia*, 7 volumes,
Angus and Robertson, 1950–1970. Here we have a record of
books about Australia published in many parts of the world,
not only in the country itself. Sir John has stated (in the fifth
volume) 'few countries of the world have so complete a record
of their origin'. Perhaps we may not see anything comparable
attempted again.

But *The British National Bibliography* is not this type of work: it
is a record of every new book *published* in Great Britain, whatever
the language, whatever the subject. If students will spend an
hour or so with an annual cumulation of BNB they will see from
the title-page that it is 'A subject list of new books published in
Great Britain, based on books received by the Agent for the
Copyright Libraries; classified, with modifications, according
to the Dewey Decimal Classification; catalogued according to
the British Text of the Anglo-American Cataloguing Rules
(1967); provided with a full author, title and subject index, and
a list of British Publishers.' Then follows the list of the ten
professional and trade associations controlling and responsible
for this publication, which is a commercial body, self-support-
ing and independent entirely of the British Museum and the
Library Association. This last observation should be well noted,
because a large minority of students state erroneously that BNB
'belongs' to the British Museum; is compiled by British Museum
staff; and I have even heard it stated that BNB is the catalogue of
the British Museum Library.

Like Whitaker's CBL, BNB is available to subscribers as a
service starting with a weekly record (published every Wednes-
day), with two *Interim Cumulations* (January–April and May–
August) and the annual volume (January–December). The
subscription for the full service now costs £36. The last Wednes-
day in the month comprises the current week's record, with

the addition of a cumulated index to the preceding three or four weeks. Whitaker's distribute BNB for the publishers.

It will have been noted that from the title-page description we may infer, correctly, that this classified record, like the author and classified records compiled for *Publishers' Weekly* described above, is compiled, not from publishers' information forms or advertisements, but actually from examination of the books.

Questions requiring descriptive statements emphasizing the differences between BNB and the trade bibliographies so far dealt with may be set. They should present no difficulty if it is remembered that BNB is arranged as a subject bibliography in classified order: that is from weekly issues to the cumulations entries are arranged not in alphabetical order by author, but in a systematic, classified order, just like BPR described above. Note well, however, that the American *Subject Guide to Books in Print*, although of course it is also a subject bibliography, is not in classified form. There the entries are arranged in what is known as 'dictionary order', from A–Z according to the subject headings, with skilfully applied and numerous sub-headings for all complicated subjects.

This may seem bewildering, but a few minutes' handling of BNB and the *Subject Guide* reveals the difference immediately. When classification is discussed in chapter seven, the specific advantages may also be obvious, although many users of catalogues always prefer the A–Z approach to subject cataloguing to the DC.

Those who use BNB must master the author, title and subject index referred to on its title page; remembering for examination and practical purposes that the indexes to the American *Subject Guide* in contrast are, in fact, the six quarto volumes of *Publishers' Trade List Annual*.

The index of BNB enables a bookseller with no knowledge of DC, not even the superficial knowledge gained by using the catalogue of the local public library, to find his way about the 2,000 pages of an average annual volume with ease and speed.

Again, it is important to read the preface to this work, for details are there given of certain publications excluded (novelettes of a minor type, Parliamentary Papers, and a few other categories) as well as some useful hints for tracing information. Every cumulated annual volume contains an outline of the classification, a list of publishers (addresses of new and minor firms are of obvious time-saving value to booksellers, as too are details of author-publishers, printer-publishers, for orders of this nature are usually best obtained direct by customers); and a selected entry in full which explains all the abbreviations. Here then, is a complete description of a book presented in the compressed, codified convention adopted and followed consistently throughout BNB. All of this should convince every student that it is unwise to consult this bibliographical record without first having read the explanatory material.

BNB started the first week in January, 1950: being then unique in the world of systematic national bibliography. The application of the highest standards of close classification, full cataloguing and indexing, have made it indispensable to librarians and to all booksellers with library business. Small firms unable to afford the subscription will always find the local library staff willing to help with queries which possibly can only be answered quickly by reference to BNB.

Cumulations published to date take the form of a *Cumulated Index* for every five-year period from 1950 (thus we have 1950–1954, 1955–1959, 1960–1964; with the latest volume for a three-year period 1965–1967).

Differentiate carefully between this *Cumulated Index* series, and the *Cumulated Subject Catalogue, 1955–1959* (published in 1963); and the earlier one for 1951–1954. The period 1955–1959 extends to three quarto volumes, which comprise the entries from individual annual volumes 're-assembled in a single sequence of subjects', thus enabling users to review five years of publishing on all subjects and to discard the annual volumes. It will be quickly understood that the key to *Cumulated Subject Catalogue, 1955–1959* is the alphabetical *Cumulated Index* for 1955–1959 described above. The published price of £24 for the three volumes, plus £9·50 for the *Index* makes this something of a luxury service for all but the largest firms, but is not expensive when one considers the work involved in compilation and printing nearly 4,000 quarto pages of such detailed, complicated information.

Considerable time is saved if the searcher is able to look up his subject enquiry, first in the *Cumulated Index*, and then noting the classification numbers of his quarry and its subdivisions, can turn at once to the *Subject Catalogue* to the pages containing entries for those numbers. The latest in this series is the *Cumulated Subject Catalogue, 1965–1967*, 2 vols., £30. For a detailed explanation see *A Description of the BNB: a manual of practice*, published by the BNB in 1971, £3.

Of little or no importance to booksellers is the complementary service of a specialized nature in a unique record, much needed, known as *The British Catalogue of Music* which started in 1957. This provides classified lists of new music with index entries 'in one alphabetical sequence of composers, arrangers, editors, authors of words, etc. The first catalogue of British music of its kind and the most comprehensive'. For this invaluable bibliography of music a special classification was evolved, complicated because of the special problems presented to classifiers and cataloguers of music who found all existing schemes unsatisfactory. Those interested should buy the complete set of tables, compiled by E. J. Coates, published by BNB., at 7/9 Rathbone Street, London, W1, from which editorial office, detailed prospectuses of all the bibliographical services now available from BNB may be obtained. Students are advised to obtain the complete set, for they are useful aids when preparing for examinations.

As explained above, the American BPR is to some extent now providing a national classified bibliography for American published books on a month by month basis. But for the full counterpart to BNB, with one special feature which not even that great enterprise offers, we must turn to the *Cumulative Book Index*, published by the H. W. Wilson Company of New York.

CBI (not to be confused with Whitaker's CBL) is wider in scope than BNB, and even more elaborate. The majority of the entries record the publication of all new books in the USA, Canada, and Great Britain. But it comprises even more than this intake: for it is nothing less than a *World List of Books in the English Language*. And this means what it says, because the purpose of CBI is to record the publication of every new book *written in the English Language*, wherever the place of publication may be, providing of course details of publisher, price (with American or British price for foreign books obtainable through an American or British agent or publisher, always named). Since 1945, English being *lingua franca* for the countries of the Commonwealth (and indeed in an astonishing number of other countries of the modern world), the foreign publication of books in the English language has greatly increased.

Scholars find learned academic theses on linguistics and the English language, scientific monographs, literary monographs, and similar specialized printed material being published as a matter of course in English in Helsinki, Oslo, Geneva, Zurich, Amsterdam, Rome, Athens; popular books on the art of flower arrangement and miniature tree culture turn up in Tokyo; historical monographs and studies in higher mathematics start their lives, in English, in Delhi; and some treatises of importance to specialists, even come from Moscow, Warsaw, and Prague. We find Eastern cook books being published in English in Beirut; substantial contributions to travel literature, literary history and biography, available only in Australia, and so on.

All such books, being published in English, are recorded in the unique world list known as CBI, not only in the body of the work, in their correct placing according to the conventional entries, but, in cumulations, in repeated entries, arranged in groups by the country of origin, at the beginning of volumes. How important this service is to searchers and specialists may be judged by the chance check I once made in a mere six-month cumulation: lengthy lists were recorded therein from no fewer than twenty-five different countries.

It is impossible, even for CBI staff, to track down every single book: but this is their ideal, for the coverage of every annual cumulation is intended to be exactly what it is subtitled: a world list.

A paragraph of historical interest will here be worth remembering: CBI started in 1898 as the *United States Catalogue* (continuing the earlier *American Catalogue* – note the parallel development of the *English Catalogue of Books* described on page 28), and the last volume entitled the *U.S. Catalogue* appeared in 1928. Thereafter the name and the scope were changed to their present form.

Many public libraries and the larger bookshops subscribe to CBI, the former benefitting, if so desired, from a complementary service consisting of a card reprint distribution either through Library of Congress Catalogue Cards, or from a publisher's series.

Subscribers to the full service receive cumulations in a series of two-monthly paperbacks; then a January–July cloth-bound quarto; and finally, the annual volume. Subsequent cumulations cover two-yearly periods, commencing with the 1957–1958 volume. A complete range of the previous cumulations would be hard to come by, being the largest and heaviest reference books in daily use in a library: marvels of accurate printing, clarity of arrangement, and consistently applied editorial skill.

Except for the largest libraries and firms, this Wilson service might be costly and even prohibitive, were it not for the policy of this unique bibliographical firm. By arrangement, the H. W. Wilson service of CBI is available on a special service basis of charge, subscription rates being quoted on request. For a full explanation of this, see Appendix 2 and for additional bibliographies published by H. W. Wilson, see the next chapter.

Cataloguing technique in CBI is virtually faultless: it is most unusual to spot a misprint or find an error. Entries are detailed, equalled only by BNB, and in some respects, even surpassing that high standard. For example, dates of authors are given, and very full descriptive details are provided under the main entries, which are those under authors' names.

Subject, title, and series entries are also provided, with liberal cross-references, added entries under translators and illustrators and the whole work is compiled with strict adherence to a cataloguing code which may well serve as a model.

One formal difference between CBI and BNB must be noted: as previously stated with emphasis, BNB is a subject bibliography, arranged systematically in the classified order of an extended Dewey Decimal scheme; but CBI on the other hand, is a dictionary catalogue: that is, the entries (comprising authors, subjects, and titles) are arranged in one alphabetical order A–Z.

A merest glance at a two-year cumulation will show how necessary it is, when dealing with so many scores of thousands of entries arranged alphabetically, to learn and apply very strictly, strict rules of alphabetization. This should make us all discard the everyday phrase 'as easy as ABC'. That is the reason for devoting a special chapter to this apparently simple exercise of arranging entries in strict alphabetical order.

In CBI, subjects attracting many books, and thus requiring much subdivision according to specific minor topics, are first arranged under the main subject headings, with numerous cross-references. For example:

BIOLOGY
History
Laboratory Manuals
Terminology
(followed by 27 cross-references)

BIRDS
Habits and Behaviour
Migration
Pictorial Works
(followed by 13 geographical headings)

Although an American invented the most widely-used book classification American cataloguers have always favoured a dictionary form of library and trade catalogue; British librarians from the Edwardian era have preferred the classified form. Many users of dictionary catalogues such as CBI dislike the hundreds of cross-references that are necessary if related subjects, separated by the accident of the alphabet, are to be linked up, finding them both tiresome and over-elaborate. The preference must be a personal choice; one soon gets used to the form of catalogue consulted frequently. What we have to clearly understand is the formal difference between CBI and BNB, remembering that when consulting the latter we must always use the index in order not to miss or overlook inter-related topics and subdivisions. Whatever the merits of BNB are, and they are very considerable, the World List coverage of CBI must never be overlooked by booksellers handling library and specialized orders.

From 1971 a new bibliographic service on ultra fiche was initiated by the Council of the BNB, called *Books in English*. Subscribers are invited to order a PCMI Reader for use when consulting the microfilms.

QUESTIONS FOR RECAPITULATION

1. Write concise descriptive notes on the following, giving in full the titles of every bibliography, and emphasizing the differences in coverage, function and detail between them:
CBL; CBI; BNB; BPR; *Books in Print; Publishers' Trade List Annual; Subject Guide to Books in Print; Publishers' Weekly; Cumulated Subject Catalogue;* BNB *Cumulated Index.*

2. What is the formal difference between a dictionary catalogue of books and a classified catalogue? Which form do you prefer, and why? Name examples of each type.

3. What is a cross-reference in cataloguing? Give two actual or imaginary examples. Why are they necessary?

4. Make a list in order of importance, of the trade and other bibliographies you regard as necessary tools of the trade for (a) medium-size bookshops; and (b) the larger bookshops with library, learned institutional, research, industrial, export and specialized customers.

5. A dictionary catalogue of books is self-indexing: why is this so? A classified catalogue must be provided with an index: why? What form must it be compiled in, if the user is to be completely satisfied with its service?

Chapter 5
Ancillary Bibliographic Aids: 1

The last decade has produced many subordinate bibliographic aids for the use of booksellers and librarians, especially for those interested either for trade or research, in scientific and technical information. Students should try to obtain Hans Zell's *New Reference Tools for Librarians*, a catalogue issued in 1964 by Robert Maxwell and Co. That this extends to 230 pages is an indication not only of the thoroughness of the book but also of the comparative wealth of material now available, although the compiler's range takes in dictionaries, encyclopaedias, documentation and other reference material as well as bibliographies.

Secondary though these may be we shall give brief attention to them here, because assistants and students working in larger shops will need to have knowledge of them if they are not to be overlooked as sources of information. Specific examples of their use in daily work will indicate their relative importance, emphasizing when it is worth the trouble to seek extra-mural help when dealing with difficult orders from important customers.

But we will first of all deal with a secondary class likely to be used in all bookshops, and to be considered as supplementary to the services of Whitaker's standard works, and of the equivalent American cumulations and trade indexes.

In a report of a working party on book trade bibliographies, presented to the May 1965 Conference of the Booksellers Association, students will find a detailed, descriptive list of everything of major and nearly everything of secondary importance in this field of our study, together with a survey of results of a questionnaire sent to 100 bookshops and 100 libraries asking for information about these works and especially for a record of stock and holdings of each title.

It was surprising to the present writer to find from this return that only two of the bookshops replying (sixty-two in all) subscribed regularly to *British Book News*, a monthly magazine edited by an official bibliographer of the British Council.

Certainly the function of *British Book News* is to assist our export trade by providing publicity for new books published in Great Britain and the Commonwealth; and to achieve this by distribution of the magazine wherever in the world there are British Council libraries and offices; but this unique publication is so authoritative and superlatively well presented that one is puzzled to learn of its neglect in Britain as a source of book information rather more reliable and of greater value than many newspaper and magazine reviews.

Subtitled 'A Guide to Book Selection', BBN (not to be confused with BNB) was started at the beginning of the last world war (1940). Each monthly issue contains a longish bibliographical survey of a specific subject (usually scientific, medical or technical, but sometimes literary) written by a specialist. The rest of each month's seventy to eighty pages consists of brief, concisely written surveys in about 250 words, of the most important and notable books of the previous month. These 'reviews' are done by members of a panel of specialists. Fiction and children's literature come within the scope of BBN, which each month includes a coloured paper insert giving advance news of forthcoming books, together with a full index.

The value of such a well-established and greatly respected guide to booksellers when recommending the best of British books to specialist and foreign customers is clearly proved by the merest glance at a random issue. Here is a specimen entry:

Bibliography

A BIBLIOGRAPHY OF THE WRITINGS OF W. B. YEATS. Allan Wade. 3rd edition revised and edited by Russell K. Alspach. *Hart-Davies*, 63s. 1968. 22.5 cm. 514 pages. Illustrations. Index. (*Soho Biographies*)

This is the third edition of the standard bibliography of Yeats's work, based on the late Allan Wade's early work of 1908, as well as that of A. J. A. Symons, W. M. Roth and P. S. O'Hegarty. The second edition was completed by Rupert Hart-Davis, as Mr Wade died when revising the first edition; the present edition has been revised by Colonel Alspach, who edited the Variorum Poems (with G. D. P. Allt) and the Variorum Plays. He has included particularly useful material from Professor Shotaro Oshima's *W. B. Yeats and*

Japan and added details to several items, as well as trying 'to make a complete listing of all publications dealing primarily with Yeats that appeared between 1957 and early 1966'. This is part of a larger task (undertaken by the late Professor K. G. W. Cross and Mr R. N. Dunlop, a vast bibliography of writings on Yeats up to 1965, which should soon go to press) and it is not complete. An important omission from the editions of Yeats's works is The Scholars Library edition, *Poems of W. B. Yeats*, first published by Macmillan (London) in 1962 and subsequently reprinted. Colonel Alspach has added to the usefulness of this bibliography in his edition.   (012)

It will be noticed by the observant that BBN is classified by DC, and is in fact a subject list. Monthly indexes (authors, titles, series) are cumulated annually as a separate issue.

Fiction sections of BBN are aids to the identification of novels ordered by hazy-minded customers without correct or full titles; they enable an assistant to compile straight on to a typewriter an order-list of, say, the year's best thrillers, historical novels, short stories. If one retains a year or two of BBN on file one will quickly be able to decide if it is worth its filing space: but, one must remember it is there to be used, and know precisely the sort of information it will yield. Why, therefore, is it so neglected by the British book trade? In coverage it surpasses anything comparable; in consistent, high quality of content it is altogether admirable.

Understandably, most booksellers have to be carefully selective in stocking for staff use, not for sale: and as one would expect, first in popularity in the secondary aids is Whitaker's *Paperbacks in Print*: a reference catalogue, printed double column, and appearing twice yearly in summer and winter editions.

This handy checklist is arranged under fifty-three categories, with author and title index. Its rapid growth from the first thin paperback to its present 836 pages (1969), listing over 35,000 paperbacks in print and on sale in Great Britain, reveals to us how vast this industry has grown in a decade. The American counterpart is just as lengthy: but note, Bowker's *Paperbound Books in Print*, is a monthly, with cumulated indexes, listing over 30,000 American paperbacks.

Two other Whitaker catalogues have firmly established themselves: *Technical and Scientific Books in Print*, which in the 1969/1970 edition lists 25,440 titles arranged in forty-five main

categories and three hundred subgroups, totalling 765 pages
(price £1·50). For some reason or other, trade cataloguers try
to avoid using Dewey but this catalogue is easy enough to
consult, provided as it is with author and title indexes. The
second Whitaker catalogue is *Children's Books in Print*: a reference
catalogue of over 14,000 children's books in print and on sale
in Great Britain (January 1969 issue). Here the entries, with
indexes, are arranged under ninety-nine main headings.

Most booksellers subscribe to the weekly Smith's *Trade News*,
for which seasonal supplements are compiled, as, for example,
an annual supplement, compiled from publishers' publicity
material, on *Children's Books*, running to over one hundred
pages, quarto magazine size.

This publicity is not selective, but it provides a useful
grouping and presentation of publishers' junior series, and of
popular juvenile books for conventional reading-age groups
from first readers through to Group 4 (10 to 16 years), for which
brief descriptive notes are provided, similar treatment being
given to Group 3, overlapping for the 8 to 12 years-of-age
children. There is a separate section for popular annuals, with
many illustrations of book jackets, the whole thing being
presented in a popular format to suit all sections of the trade.

Other special numbers of *Trade News* presented in the same
style are *Maps and Atlases, Travel Guides, Bibles, Gardening Books,
Cook Books*. All are worth keeping for reference for at least six
months after issue.

Turning once more to the USA book industry, we should
remember *News of Books*: 'an evaluation of Adult Books and a
listing of Juvenile Books, as an aid to retail buyers, public
librarians, school librarians.' It is a monthly issued by Ancorp
National Services, Inc., of New York, an organization with
twenty-four branches in the USA and Canada. Its only feature is
a listing captioned *The Month*, with entries arranged first by date
of publication (from publishers' advance handouts) and then
under titles, with long, fifty- to one hundred-word annotations,
prefixed by assessment symbols: U = Unpredictable, F = Fair,
G = Good, E = Excellent, with, not without heart-burnings,
doubtless, an uncertain ? – 'dunno' as the uncooperative,
questioned opinion poll makers and shapers of things to come so
wisely murmur.

Oh! But they have so many aids in the vast American book

industry that one wonders if and why booksellers and librarians ever make bad judgments: perhaps they never do. Why, they have 'quick access to 2,425 Juvenile Book Reviews' in just one year's issue of *School Library Journal Book Review*, all arranged under DC, with age-level for every reviewed book. It is fully indexed, even by illustrators, and as an annual no doubt is one of the R. R. Bowker Company's lesser publications though greatly valued, especially by librarians.

Every bookseller will doubtless have his own favourites amongst these too many choices, but few who know it will overlook the outstandingly useful list from our own City of London Guildhall Library of the hundreds of trade, town, financial and commercial directories available in the superlatively well-stocked Commercial Library in the City of London. So comprehensively world-wide is the coverage in Guildhall, EC4, that one may well conclude that if they do not have it there, then it doesn't exist.

Turning now to other ancillary bibliographical aids, we should consider Author Bibliographies.

The compiler of an author bibliography should provide a complete record of everything his author published. Scope and style of presentation may vary, depending very much on the complexity of the author's output. Such works, of great value to book collectors, literary historians, reference librarians and antiquarian booksellers, only occasionally help general booksellers, who may wish to refer to them in public libraries in order to provide a specialist customer with information.

Published works are recorded in author bibliographies in the fullest detail, copied from title-pages, and set out in a conventional style established by such men as Thomas James Wise (1859–1937) whose strange career is now notorious because of the sensational revelations which started in Carter and Pollard's *An Enquiry into the Nature of Certain Nineteenth Century Pamphlets* (Constable, 1934), finding echoes in all the great private and other libraries of America. This is an amusing and fascinating theme of its own, and students who are interested in bibliographical detective investigations should read Carter and Pollard on Wise and his methods.

Author bibliographies are conveniently arranged in chronological order of date of first publication. This arrangement enables a literary critic and historian to trace the pattern of an author's development from firstlings to mature work; from the products of his nonage to those of his last years.

It is well to know and to memorize a few famous examples: the specimen entry illustrating the style of a BBN review (see page 42–3) provides one standard author bibliography which, it will be seen, has gone into three editions in spite of its price and comparatively limited public. The current back list of Rupert Hart-Davis will list all available *Soho Bibliographies*, the most notable series of its kind in postwar publishing, which includes classical works such as *Rupert Brooke*, by the doyen of British bibliographers, Sir Geoffrey Keynes, and a superb piece of work in the *Henry James* of Leon Edel and Dan H. Laurence.

Three to five pounds may seem a high price for such books, but one must remember that their preparation entails years of arduous research, and that because of the limited market, editions are probably limited also, to a thousand copies or even less. The *Henry James* is an example of a bibliography of great complexity, for James's literary output was vast and included many fugitive contributions to magazines, revisions of early texts, and moreover, was published in both New York and London. His writings included in the standard collected edition extend to no fewer than twelve large volumes of short stories (Hart-Davis); many novels; *novelle*, travel literature, essays, literary and art criticism, biography, autobiography, plays, and correspondence: truly the literary life at high level by one who was perhaps the most 'unpopular' great writer of his time.

Apart from the pleasure of knowing that such a bibliography exists, of what practical use is it to a general bookseller? The answer is, very little. Yet I have known when it was necessary to consult a public reference library copy for a foreign customer who wished to buy volumes containing a selection of specified short stories only.

The same sort of enquiry required reference to another author bibliography, namely *Rudyard Kipling: a bibliographical catalogue*, by James McG. Stewart (OUP, 1959, 694 pp.). Similarly, *Joseph Conrad*, a biographical study by Jocelyn Baines, Weidenfeld and Nicolson, 1960, contains a complete list of the short stories by this prolific writer in that form, in alphabetical order.

One further example may be memorized: *Jane Austen: a critical bibliography*, by R. W. Chapman (OUP, 1955). This is a small work (72 pp.) but it is mentioned here because it provides an example of a 'critical' approach to an author's texts. As R. W. Chapman was acknowledged to be the greatest 'Janeite' of his own, and perhaps of all time, his work is of the greatest importance not only to collectors of first and early editions, but also to literary historians and editors.

Many other examples may be seen in the *Oxford General Catalogue*, where they are listed at DC 012; and one should not overlook the select author bibliographies which are a familiar feature of the well-known British Council series of critical monographs: *Writers and their Work*, of which there are now over two hundred. Published for the British Council by Longman, as supplements to BBN, at the very low price of 17½p, these paperbacks are all written by well-known critics and biographers whose task it is to provide biographical summaries of classic and standard living British writers, a critical appreciation of their books, and a selective bibliography. Everything of importance and general interest is recorded with dates of first publication, but no claim for completeness is made. Finally, a list of books about the writer is given. The standard is high and the series has done a great deal to spread knowledge of British writers abroad. Note recent additions, dealing not with one writer, but with topics in English Literature such as *English Maritime Writing: Hakluyt to Cook ; English Translators and Translations ; Cavalier Poets ; English Travellers in the Near East.*

I would like to know that every bookshop in the land possessed a complete set of this first-class series at such a give-away cost: but must admit to disappointment and astonishment when I read the result of a Booksellers Association working party's survey. However, when dealing with a certain type of specific enquiry or compiling a buying list for a good customer, don't overlook *British Writers and their Work* and when helping a college or public library to build up basic stock, make it a resolution not to rest until you have sold a complete set.

QUESTIONS FOR RECAPITULATION

1. Describe BBN, stressing its usefulness to the British book trade.

2. List all the ancillary bibliographic aids published regularly

by J. Whitaker and by American firms providing similar service to booksellers.

3. What information does an author bibliography provide the researcher? Name two examples; and show how they might be useful to book customers and to booksellers.

4. What do you know of the work of the British Council for British books, other than the publication of BBN?

Chapter 6
Ancillary Bibliographic Aids: 2

Passing references have been made to subject bibliographies because these are more likely to be useful to booksellers than author bibliographies. The most widely used example in the trade is Whitaker's *Technical Books in Print*, previously described. Many of the articles in *British Book News* take the form of subject bibliographies with a commentary by a subject specialist. In a general survey I have dealt with hundreds of such bibliographies in the October, November, and December, 1968 issues of this magazine, arranging those mentioned in DC order for convenience. This series also dealt with dictionaries and glossaries of technical terms as an associated group of reference books.

It has been pointed out that the catalogue of Mendelssohn's collection of books relating to South Africa is an example of a subject bibliography. Here it is emphasized that in practice the catalogue of any special library is a subject bibliography. Hence the importance of remembering this simple fact if you are searching for details of books on specific subjects. Consider, for example, the catalogue of H. K. Lewis's commercial lending library for doctors and scientists, technologists and specialists, which includes details of a standard stock of new books, British and American. True, being a bookseller's and publisher's own trade list, the full details are not given, but dates and published prices are. The parent volume (1950) of this great collection extends to 1,152 pages, with subject references, because the arrangement is by authors' surnames, A–Z. There are supplements every few years; and the whole set is well worth buying, because it serves as a very quick reference guide to very specialized books. When the year of publication is known, your search is narrowed and speeded up, because you can proceed direct to the *Cumulative Book List* or *English Catalogue* if the book is published in Great Britain; if not, to the American *Books in Print*. Eventually you may have to consult the publisher's current

4

stock lists. But more of this in the chapter on the method of search.

Subject bibliographies abound: consult the *General Catalogue* of the Oxford University Press under Dewey number 016; and if you have access to it, BNB. Memorize a few good examples of different kinds, such as, in addition to those described above, *Bibliography of British History* in progress (published by OUP for the Royal Historical Society of Great Britain, and the American Historical Association); *English Literature, 1660–1800: a Bibliography of Modern Studies* compiled for *Philological Quarterly* (Princeton, 1950); the great catalogue of the library of the London School of Economics and Political Science, noting that the point made above about catalogues of libraries is here emphasized by the fact that LSE entitle the work *A London Bibliography of the Social Sciences.* This multi-volumed record may be consulted in the larger reference libraries. It answers many queries from export customers, foreign universities, and foreign librarians.

A bibliography dealing with subjects, unlike an author bibliography, is seldom complete. Subjects are too vast, and have no finality, except in the fields of antiquity. One could have a complete bibliography of works on alchemy; but complete coverage of a subject such as chemistry would be in practice both impossible and of little value.

A select bibliography of a very special kind, and a standard work for decades, was entitled *The Best Books*, in five quarto volumes, by William Swan Sonnenschein (later Stallybrass). The index volume to the third revision, and, alas, the last, was published by Routledge in 1935, together with a synopsis to the classification, for this gigantic work of 3,384 pages was an evaluative, subject bibliography, arranged on a scheme of bibliographical classification evolved by the great bibliographer himself. Nothing like this had been done before and nothing like it will ever be done again. Those libraries and bookshops that possess the set have a work of reference still of very great practical value. Yet I have seen it pushed aside as outdated. Certainly it is, but Sonnenschein's industry was astonishingly productive; his assessments of permanent use. We cannot linger to turn the pages of this remarkable bibliographic aid, but one example must be quoted: in 1950 one of the Hutchinson group of publishers reprinted a book entitled *Weather-lore: a garner of traditions*, first published in 1869, second enlarged edition 1898, after which it appeared to be forgotten. The author was Richard Inwards. Look it up in Part 1 of Sonnenschein, page 368, and there you will find it, asterisked and evaluated as 'the fullest and most interesting work on the subject'. Now such information about a book nearly a century old is of practical use to a buyer. Subscription orders for the reprint soon cleared his stock, for *Weather-lore* soon went o.p. Assistants who work in antiquarian bookshops will find Sonnenschein useful when called upon to estimate the chances of selling older books offered for purchase, because *Best Books* abounds in similar examples of perception and knowledge on the part of the compiler. The bibliographer cast his net very wide, scouring the American book scene for first-class contributions to specific subjects, and even bringing books from Rome, Paris, Berlin, Hanoi, and India, within his catch. I remember being asked to trace and supply a book on some strange Eastern doctrine and occult experiences for a customer who resented my answer: 'regret cannot trace or identify this book'. 'But,' he wrote, 'it is mentioned in a footnote by Aldous Huxley in . . .' (naming that encyclopaedic writer's latest non-fiction book at that time). This spurred me on to take a glance at Sonnenschein in a last attempt: sure enough, it was there, annotated, and with publication details taking one back a century or more, to India. At least one was able to pass on this information to settle the query. So, Sonnenschein's work must never be dismissed as 'out-of-date', nor should his contribution to select, evaluative bibliography ever be underestimated, forgotten, or depreciated.

An example of a bibliographical record on the grand scale is the *Cambridge Bibliography of English Literature*, first edited by Frederick W. Bateson, five volumes, 1940–1957. The last volume of 1957 was a supplement edited by George Watson. This vast compilation is under revision, and vols 2 and 3 (1660–1800; 1800–1900), fully revised and enlarged by George Watson have now been published, 1969 and 1971, £10; £13. Vol. 4 of the original set is an index. To clarify this, memorize the details thus:

> CBEL: 5 vols.—1: 600–1660; 2: (revised): 1660–1800;
> 3: (revised): 1800–1900;
> 4: *Index;* 5: *Supplement*

Assistants working in shops where orders for older books are filled for literary and learned institutions will frequently require the help of CBEL and antiquarians of the book trade must certainly use it almost daily. All students should spend some time consulting it at the local reference library.

The aim of the compilers of CBEL is to provide a record 'as far as possible in chronological order' of the authors, titles, and editions, 'with relevant critical matter, of all writings in book form (whether in English or Latin) that can still be said to possess some literary interest, by natives of what is now (that was, in 1940) the British Empire, up to the year 1900'.

The supplementary volume records works published between 1935 and 1955 relating to subjects and authors in the bibliographies contained in the parent work, which grew out of the bibliographies in the *Cambridge History of English Literature*, fifteen volumes (1907–1916) reprinted without this feature, price £2 each volume.

Reverting to CBEL note that the index volume is a subject index; that is to say, authors are here treated as subjects when their books are listed in the main bibliographies. Authors of the critical and biographical monographs, however, have not so far been indexed, nor have the titles of books, except, of course, for anonyma. Doubtless machine compilation methods now available will speed up the complete indexing of this wonderfully useful reference work.

When students leaf through the library copy they might note how the index volume to the parent work (vol. 4) is also made to serve as an index to the supplementary volume, vol. 5.

Although it must be allowed that CBEL is normally for the aristocrats and the antiquarians of the trade, it is to be hoped that every thoughtfully equipped bookshop, however small, is provided with a staff copy of George Watson's the *Concise Bibliography of English Literature, 600–1950*, CUP, 1958; revised second edition 1965 (£1·25 cloth; paperback 62½p). Although this is an abridgment, note the extension to 1950 in the date limits. The handy book we now have provides probably all the information normally required by the book trade about books published by authors from the pre-Chaucerian period to 1950. The new arrangement of entries is also easier to cope with in the hurry of a day's work in a busy shop. The parent work demands the quiet and leisure of the library.

The *Concise CBEL* has a general introduction relating to reference books, collections, and bibliographies, followed by author bibliographies arranged alphabetically, instead of chronologically as in the parent work, in six periods: *The Old English Period* (A.D. 600–1100); *The Middle English Period* (1100–1500); *The Renaissance to the Restoration* (1500–1660); *The Restoration to the Romantics* (1660–1800); *The Nineteenth Century* (1800–1900); and finally, the new section *The Early Twentieth Century* (1900–1950). About 400 authors are admitted, of which 80 belong to the present century. The editor has been able to include in his author index references to the biographical and critical monographs recorded. This is a most useful feature. To give students a clear impression of the type of entry, attention is drawn to an average example, namely, under Oscar Wilde, page 197. There you will find the details of the 1908–1914 bibliography of Wilde; followed by a list of his books with dates of first editions; notable later editions; an entry for the 14 volumes of collected 'Works'; the selection by Aldington; and then references to three well-known books on Wilde: Frank Harris's (1918 and 1938); Hesketh Pearson's (1946); and St John Ervine's unusually critical book (1951). Clearly, every bookseller and all students should be familiar with the *Concise CBEL*.

Because it has been compiled with the needs of the book trade in mind, the present writer's *An English Library* (André Deutsch, 1963, £1·50 cloth; 30p paperback) should be mentioned here. This 'Bookman's Guide' is fully explained in the introduction to the last revision and has the added feature of providing details regarding the best and standard editions available, with publishers, of all the books recorded and described from *Beowulf* to Virginia Woolf, Dr G. M. Trevelyan and other contemporaries whose recent death has brought them within the scope of the work, for no living writers are included. *An English Library* enables the bookseller to answer quickly, without reference to other books, such everyday enquiries as: 'What editions of Blake's *Poems* are available? What is the reading order for the *Palliser* series of novels? What twentieth-century autobiographies could be recommended as likely to remain permanent classics, and what editions are usually available? Is there a cheaper edition of Dorothy Osborne's *Letters* than Moore Smith's definitive collection?

What are the contents of the book entitled *Barnstormer Plays*, why were they so called, and where can I get them?' – and so on.

Students are referred to the last section of *An English Library* for fuller treatment of bibliographical and other aids likely to be useful to booksellers. Some are so important that they must be considered here. For example, D. C. Browning's *Dictionary of Literary Biography* revised in 1960 for Dent's *Everyman Reference Library*. The new edition covers American as well as British material; the 2,300 literary biographies give titles and dates of principal works of authors, of which 650 relate to the twentieth century.

With characteristic American thoroughness and bibliographical competence, the single volume formerly known as Bessie Graham's *Bookman's Manual*, a mine of information for generations of bookmen, has now grown to encyclopaedic coverage in two volumes, with a new title: *The Reader's Adviser*, 11th edition, R. R. Bowker, 1969. This 'biographical, critical and bibliographical' reference work should be known to all bookmen: trade, professional and general readers, as well as university, college and school students.

Volume 1 is a guide to the best in literature ($22·00); volume 2 is described as a layman's guide to the best in general biography, history, bibles, world religions, philosophy, psychology, the sciences, folklore, the lively arts, communications, and travel ($20·35).

One soon acquires the habit of consulting it with the greatest respect and gratitude. So complicated is this world of books that such an atlas of bibliographic description is a secondary or ancillary reference book to be recommended to those customers who are librarians, both private and public; to export customers supplying and stocking great new libraries for the English-speaking world; to students of the open university; to academic and teaching staff. It should be available in every public reference library. The tradesman will then be able to send his likely customers to the *Reader's Adviser* as to an encyclopaedia and a polymath. As Sydney Smith said of Whewell, so we may say of the editor (and his staff): 'Science was his forte; omniscience his foible.'

European writers of eminence, including scholars, poets, novelists, playwrights, from over twenty countries, are the subject of an admirable addition to *Everyman's Reference Library* published in 1968: *Everyman's Dictionary of European Writers*, by W. N. Hargreaves-Mawdsley. This is a companion to D. C. Browning's English and American *Dictionary of Literary Biography* mentioned above, and is the same price (£1·90). For a book of 576 pages, containing references 'ranging from briefer notices on minor figures to full-scale articles on major authors', this is a handy work for all larger shops to have in the staff library.

Somewhat more ambitious is a new survey in a series of critical and biographical introductions which Martin Seymour-Smith has been engaged on for many years: a *Guide to Modern World Literature* extending to about half a million words. The coverage is here so comprehensive that the historical and literary references are to every modern writer of importance since 1900, with a glance back to those writers whose work has exercised great influence on the moderns. The work will be published in 1972.

One must not neglect books dealing with children's literature of note, especially those with the critical approach, lacking, of course, in the trade catalogues, such as *Children's Books in Print* and *Trade News Children's Books* described above. The best detailed treatment will be found in Margery Fisher's excellent and most readable *Intent Upon Reading* (Brockhampton Press) which offers 'a critical appraisal of modern fiction for children'. A companion work, *Matters of Fact*, being a study of aspects of non-fiction for children was announced in 1971. *Intent Upon Reading* is attractively produced with illustrations, a good index, and is now an established guide to over 1,500 books by 750 authors. With a copy handy in the children's section of a well-stocked bookshop few assistants would be unable to recommend suitable stories for all age groups with confidence.

Students are sometimes asked to make a list with descriptive annotations of books suitable for school libraries. Here then, is a helpful pointer to a satisfactory choice for such questions.

In this brief survey I have given examples of only a few specialized sources of bibliographical information, but selective as this choice is, it makes plain to those working in many types of bookshop what is available to assist them in daily work; and to help the customer whose enquiries may range from, 'What's new in my line?' to 'Can you select for me . . .?' (here the request may vary from 'a library' to 'half a dozen books on . . .').

Reference to other aids will be made in other chapters on the general technique of the search for books and information, and in part three: *Notes on a Knowledge of Stock.*

Booksellers with many important foreign customers, and the largest firms offering a highly specialized and comprehensive service, will as a matter of course be familiar with the remarkable development of national trade book records, following the model established in Britain and the United States. Thus we now have *Australian Books in Print, Canadian Books in Print, German Books in Print, Italian Books in Print,* and a listing of books received by the French National Library Depository in the recent *Bibliographie de la France.*

QUESTIONS FOR RECAPITULATION

1. List six subject bibliographies which you think would be useful as reference books in large bookshops serving academic and other educational customers.

2. Outline the scope and arrangement of the *Cambridge Bibliography of English Literature.* What is recorded in the latest supplementary volume? What features of the index volume are noteworthy?

3. List as many titles as you can remember in Dent's *Everyman Reference Library.*

4. Write brief descriptive annotations for *The Reader's Adviser*; *Intent Upon Reading,* by Margery Fisher; and *An English Library.*

Chapter 7
The Classification of Books

Frequent references have been made in previous chapters to book classification and classified catalogues, with specific mention of the American system known all over the world as DC (Dewey's Decimal Classification). Up to about 1950 a working knowledge of DC was regarded as unnecessary for publishers and booksellers. It was recognized as part of a librarian's training, and was used by millions of children and adults who were members of school and public libraries where the system was applied in the arrangement of books on the shelves, and in the various forms of library catalogues, whether on cards, in printed form, or in typed slips filed in sheaf holders; but it was still widely ignored, even scorned, by the book trade.

But in the world of the 1970's DC is applied to business, industry, information retrieval systems, office papers, and, in its scientific extension, known as UDC (Universal Decimal Classification) by scientists requiring minute subdivisions of specialized topics. The latter development dates from 1895 and is sometimes called the Brussels Extension, because it started there. A swift glance at the latest tables in just one technical class, such as *Metallurgy* (published in Britain by the Iron and Steel Institute) reveals the astonishing complexity and range of science and technology confronting the modern student and practitioner.[1]

Classification is now a subject included in the syllabus of the diploma examination sponsored by the Booksellers Association. Now that booksellers have become familiar with DC through using BNB and BBN and American bibliographies described in chapter three, a few of the larger publishing firms have had their

1. Abridged tables are published by British Standards Institute (1961), an introduction to which, by Jean M. Perreault, was published by Clive Bingley in 1969 (£1.25) in the *Programmed Texts in Library and Information Science* series.

back lists classified. This is a development to be welcomed, and it should encourage all firms with extensive catalogues of standard books to adopt the Dewey scheme.

Itself an Education is the title of a series of lectures by B. I. Palmer on classification generally. It describes without inflation the contemporary view of the subject not only in librarianship but also in science and some sections of commerce. The superlative merits of the *Oxford General Catalogue*, in which the entries are classified by the Dewey scheme, are the best advertisement to the book trade of the application of this widely used system to academic publishing; and the increasing use of BNB should help to make classification the rule rather than as now, the exception.

The chapter on this subject in the 1964 edition of this textbook was a forecast of interest to come; now, in the 1970's, it is an essential stage in the bookseller's education. In this revision I shall therefore explain the principles of classification, the function and use of bibliographical schemes in general, and the application in particular of Dewey to trade bibliography.

Students may come across references to other schemes, such as Bliss, Brown, Library of Congress and UDC. These do not concern us here, but those who are interested will find them explained in the many textbooks stocked at all public libraries.

We become aware of classification on entering all large stores, such as Harrods, Woolworths, Marks and Spencers, where commodities are displayed in sections according to their nature and use. The larger groups are then subdivided. Thus in the clothing group we have outerwear and underwear, and within these subgroups, still further obvious divisions. This is a simple example of the first principle of all schemes, which is to separate the like from the unlike, and to group related subjects together in some sort of logical sequence.

Students will find Dewey just as simple to understand, for its application is orderly and clarifying, whether it be to books, catalogues, bibliographies, scientific papers, or office papers and correspondence. Even a few thousand unclassified books is an example of chaos and disorder. The same collection classified, one of cosmos: an orderly universe of knowledge in book form.

Dewey has its faults and approximations making it unsatisfactory for a collection of books exceeding about 250,000 volumes or for a highly specialized scientific and technical collection. Hence the Library of Congress (LC) scheme, which was evolved for the great collection there, and UDC, mentioned above, which was drawn up for the use of scientists and information librarians responsible for the classification of books, cuttings, précis and scientific papers.

But because of its comparative simplicity and the almost limitless possibilities of expansion of its decimal notation DC is ubiquitous in North America, Great Britain and the Commonwealth.

To repeat the first object of all classification schemes which I referred to above when commenting on the arrangement of goods offered for sale in large stores, let us remember that the schedules or tables, whether they are applied to knowledge or to books, must present an arrangement of subjects in an approximately logical order, bringing like things together or near each other, subdividing in a consistent pattern which separates the like from the unlike, and throughout this process proceeding from terms of great extension to terms of lesser extension until the specific is reached.

This method of progression should allow for expansion and extension of the tables when this is needed because of the discovery of new facts and the development of subjects by inventions and researches. No scheme which did not provide this flexibility could survive as a practical classification suitable for the twentieth century. Book classifications must also have the additional characteristic of a notational scheme of symbols which will facilitate the arrangement of books on the shelves, of entries in catalogues and of material in the files.

The classification of knowledge belongs to philosophy and logic. It is a mental exercise as ancient as Greek philosophy. In the third century the Neoplatonist Porphyry (*d.* A.D. 304) produced a simple division of the universe into Animate Matter; Inanimate Matter; proceeding from these headings to subdivide into other specific groups. Carl Linné (that is, Linnaeus), the Swedish botanist, from about 1738 produced his celebrated *Systema Naturae Fundamenta Botanica*, a classification of the whole plant world which is the classical foundation upon which botanical nomenclature of today has been developed. The subject has engaged the attention of thinkers in every century, and these are but two landmarks to be remembered.

The world of books is a world of infinite knowledge, complicated by the fact that books seldom fit tidily into precise
compartments of that knowledge. Scientific monographs are
usually concerned with one, named branch of science: their
classification is likely to be more precise than other classes. It is
often difficult to ascertain with absolute certainty the precise
subject of many modern books, but that is what the classifier
must do before he attempts to apply any scheme of book
classification. What then, you may ask, does he do with 'general'
books, such as encyclopaedias, which by their name indicate the
multi-subject nature of their contents. The answer is that
schemes of book classification always provide a 'Generalia' class
for such books, and for associated topics, such as bound volumes
of magazines, newspapers, and journalism. In DC this first,
general class bears the symbols 000, subdivided to provide places
for *Encyclopaedias* at 030; *General Periodicals* at 050; *Journalism* at
070; *Collected Works of Authors* (such as Ruskin and De Quincey,
who wrote on many subjects, at 081; and also for books such as
Bibliography in the Bookshop, which will be classed at 010.

The nine main classes that follow divide all human knowledge and speculation about the unknown; thus making the
complete schema one of ten divisions. Each main class is then
divided into ten subgroups; each subgroup into ten small
groups (using the term 'small' to indicate that the field of
knowledge covered is smaller in these sub-subgroups than those
above them). By the use thereafter of a decimal point (·) each of
these small groups can then be subdivided again, and so on until
a specific topic is reached, minute enough in coverage to satisfy
the classifier. Some subjects need more subdivision than others;
some classifiers require a greater degree of precision to meet
their individual needs than other users.

These main classes following the Generalia group are not
arranged haphazardly: there is an elementary logical development making them easy to remember; and there are other
mnemonic features throughout the tables, making it possible for
skilled classifiers and experienced users, to allot from memory the
correct symbols to many subjects, and to subdivide accurately.

Thus, as we have seen, 'o' is the symbol for our General
Class; and throughout the scheme a final 'o' on a main class
indicates 'General Treatment of a Class'. This final 'o' is often
discarded in practice for economy. Examples will be given later.

Meanwhile, the orderly progression of the scheme should be memorized, from

Class 100 (Philosophy)

Class 200 (Religion)

Class 300 (the Social Sciences; sometimes known as Sociology)

Class 400 (Linguistics, sometimes in earlier decades known as Languages; Dictionaries; Grammars)

Class 500 (Pure Science; the old term Natural Philosophy meant speculation about all scientific matters – except chemistry)

Class 600 (Applied Science and Technology; formerly termed the Useful Arts)

Class 700 (The Fine Arts and Recreation, including sports, and ironically the destructive 'sports' such as shooting and hunting)

Class 800 (Literature – this is the class where form is paramount)

and Class 900 (History, including Geography, and Biography – you may recall Emerson's essay on History: 'There is properly no history; only biography')

The elementary logic of the progression is plain: from creation and primitive thought, to man's intellectual speculation and belief in a deity and the development of religious beliefs; from primitive man's need to live in and as a community, bringing with it all the social sciences: law and disorder, wars, and commerce for trading; customs, costumes and folklore, to his early and perpetual need for communication, leading to the development of languages; from speculation about the natural world, the heavens, the nature of matter, chemistry, the world of rocks and minerals, of plants, and animals, to the application of all those subjects to the manufacture of useful things, the building and making arts, carpentry, and masonry; and finally, with man's need after work for recreation, the creation of art for art's sake, beginning with cavemen's pictures; with his early desire to pass on his knowledge, his reflections, and his songs, as expressed in the various literary forms. To end the scheme, we have last of all the record of 'this strange eventful history', including 'the history of particular men's lives' (as Dryden defined biography), and the story of man's exploration of the earth we live on, and its description, called geography and topography.

Having fixed the pattern of the scheme from 000 to 999 firmly in the mind, let us take a glance at one complete subdivision, to see how the thing works out in practice. If you can examine in a library a copy of the Standard (15th) Edition of Decimal Classification, do so; later editions are much more detailed, and more difficult to grasp. Turn to pages 183–4; you will see that the first subgroup 500–509 is subdivided by the *'Form Divisions'* which are common to all the main classes, to be used whenever 'consideration of the form or style in which the book is written, as well as the subject, is important' (see the introduction, page xiii for further explanation). Here all that I need to emphasize is that since some books are arranged in dictionary *form* – for example we are familiar with dictionaries of medicine; dictionaries of history, dictionaries of science – in which the material is not presented systematically by the author but in the form of articles arranged by subjects A–Z, Dewey makes provision for us to indicate this by form divisions. Thus 503 is shorthand for 'A Dictionary of Pure Science'; 603 for 'A Dictionary of Applied Science'; 703 for 'A Dictionary of Art', and 803 for 'A Dictionary of World or International Literature'. Throughout the scheme, regard the notation (that is the numbers attached to subjects) as a kind of shorthand, allowing for infinite expansion and development as human knowledge grows. Now the second subgroup, 510–519, is devoted to *Mathematics*; so a book on mathematics as a whole is classed at 510 (note the final digit, indicating general treatment of the subject). Algebra, being a topic under mathematics, will logically be located near the parent subject; it is: you will find it at 512. Now Determinants, being a branch of algebra should be allotted a place in this specific hierarchy. It is: at 512.8. And so on.

Definitions of terms such as 'determinants' and similar examples of the specialized vocabulary of mathematicians will be found in the *Elementary Scientific and Technical Dictionary*, a Longman reference book published in 1962, and it will be noted that this very work is classified by librarians at 603, as explained above in the explanation of 'forms' in the Dewey scheme.

It will be plain by now to all students how the system works out in practice. One subject; one number; subjects thus separated each from the other, but like subjects grouped near each other; unlike subjects separated by their degrees of unlikeness, and their natural characteristics. As you begin to learn

DC by using it, you will find the process of classifying is in itself an aid to mental clarity. If you arrange the bibliographies and bibliographical papers, lists and catalogues, in your 'search' department or office, by DC, you will see that everything is self-indexing, and because 820 always means the same thing (English Literature) it will automatically bring together in your office *The Oxford Companion to English Literature*; CBEL; *An English Library*; and that Cassell's *Encyclopaedia of Literature*, will be near those books, but, being international, will precede them at 803 (again note the *form* mnemonic, meaning dictionary treatment).

You will soon acquire the habit of translating the meaning of a class number or symbol, and will know without looking at some books or even handling them, quite a lot about their make-up. This facility is developed by technical librarians and information officers in great industrial firms to an uncanny degree of skill. If a technical librarian is used to classified files of technical papers, journals, abstracts of scientific material, films, cuttings, and research notes on his firm's special interests, he will probably translate his intricate UDC class numbers at sight: knowing at a glance, that a cutting in the file located at 678.84.003 not only deals with silicone production, but is limited to the financial aspects of the subject. But booksellers using bibliographies classified by the simpler DC, and applying it to their search offices, do not need to be able to classify. This calls for special training, much experience, and for mental processes which could themselves be classed at 161 and 162 (induction; scientific method; deduction; methods of reasoning, of agreement, of difference). Essential requirements of booksellers and publishers may be met by learning how the scheme works, and thus, how to find the way about BNB and similar classified records, by means of subject arrangement, with the index as a quick reference aid to location.

Those who recall the catalogue of Allen and Unwin's standard back list (of university publisher's quality) up to the 1962 issue, may agree that the index was rather a muddle because it was unsystematic. The catalogue is arranged under authors. But when the user wished to find quickly this distinguished firm's contributions to specific subjects the index was unsatisfactory.

But from 1963 onwards, the index is admirably arranged, because the entries have been arranged in DC order. Thus, supposing one wishes to ascertain or check up on Allen and

Unwin's coverage of linguistics (one of the firm's specialities), one turns at once to the number entries for 400. The 1970 catalogue listed no fewer than fourteen books on the study of language.

Moreover, due to this orderly arrangement of the index, the group 400 is followed by entries for all other books on related subjects: specific languages, books on punctuation, foreign dictionaries, letter writing, and so on, in logical sequence. Upon the muddle of the former index has been imposed the known pattern, the order, of a well-known classification scheme.

Let me give one further example: you receive an urgent telephone call for the title, publisher and price of 'a new book published three or four months ago', title forgotten; subject remembered – unusual feat on the part of the customer – it was 'a book about Fernando of Aragon and a queen of Castile', 'it was commended by Dr A. L. Rowse'; yes, you do remember the book, something about Philip the Handsome, and a mad Juana; but alas, the hundreds of later books that have passed through your office, or shop, and mind, have driven the precise details to depths which will not release the information required. If you have to search vaguely through catalogues and weekly lists, monthly cumulations, etc., you will certainly have to ring off, and spend a little time on the query, calling your enquirer later, or perhaps, be impelled to dismiss the enquiry. But if you have all your papers, lists, etc., relating to books, classified by DC, or subscribe to BNB, or keep a file of classified BBN, you will know in a flash that 946 is the DC number for history of Spain; you will turn to your file under that number, and in a second will be able to tell your enquirer that the book he wants is entitled *The Castles and the Crown* (a subject-concealing title, but the book does have an explanatory subtitle); author: Townsend Miller; publisher: Gollancz.

Meanwhile, there is a little more to describe about the mnemonic feature of DC: the method of using it; and in particular to its application in BNB and the catalogues of a few enlightened publishers. First, the national numbers. Turn to the Language Class (400) and look at the divisions of this group into specific languages. Notice that the English Language is 420; break this down mentally by saying 4 means Language Study; 42 means English Language Study; 420 means English Language Study: general books. Now if you will look under class

800, you will find that books on English Literature will take the number 820. The common digit '2' between 420 and 820 should be established in your mind as forming part of the national number for Great Britain. Test it by turning to class 900: History; subdivided to 940: European History. If '2' is a true mnemonic the number 942 should be the class denoting 'England'. It is; thus enabling you as a user of the scheme to translate the meaning of certain symbols, whenever they are used in this 'national' connotation.

Once this feature is thoroughly understood, it becomes a time-saver. You want to consult BNB, or BBN, or the *Oxford Catalogue* to choose a few new books on, say, the Economic History of England; or, something on the Political History of England. You know that 330 is DC for Economics; and 320 for Politics: therefore without wasting time on consulting indexes, you will turn quickly and without fumbling in all three reference books to 330.942; and 320.942. It will be found that other countries are treated in the same way: 943: Germany; 430: German Language; 830: German Literature, the digit '3' associated always in this respect with Germany. When '3' is used as a form symbol, it means, of course, something quite different: Dictionaries, as we have seen.

There are far too many other features in the system for me to deal with here; but three others are so useful to booksellers that they must be explained briefly, leaving a note on their application to the workaday problems to a later chapter. The first concerns the classification of biography, evolved with ingenuity and simplicity, and demanding nothing more from the user than a memory of main subject numbers. If students have access to a volume of BNB they will see at a glance, on looking up Biographies: 920, in the cumulations, that books written in this *Form*, are subdivided by the *Subject* associated with the person written about; or, in the autobiographical volumes, associated with the authors writing their own life stories. To build up the DC number for a biography, then, all we need to do is to remember 92 (omit the final digit 'o' as superfluous in this division) and then add the subject number, inserting a decimal point after the third digit from the left. Hence a biography of a doctor (for example, Harvey Cushing's classic life of Sir William Osler) is classed at 926.1. Broken down this denotes 92; plus the number for *Medicine* which is 610, omitting

5

the final digit 'o' as redundant, joining on to 92, and inserting the decimal point. Again, as Painting (Art) is 759, and as Spain is 946, Spanish Painting is 759.6 (following the method outlined above); now when we wish to classify the biography, for example, of Picasso, we immediately know without reference, that the DC number must therefore be 92 . . . add 759 . . . add 6 . . . insert decimal: resulting in 927.596.

The second feature is the classification by national numbers, of fiction. Fiction is, again, a form; and here the form in which the author has presented his material is paramount; therefore if we wish to classify fiction, as BNB does, we place all British fiction under the national subdivision following the form. Thus British fiction is arranged alphabetically under authors in the group 823, followed by *period* numbers. I have not mentioned these before, but in class 800 they are essential in order to obtain a chronological progression through the centuries. So we get 823 reserved for critical and historical monographs on British Fiction, books on 'The Novel', and the development of The Short Story as another fictional form. This group will be followed by 823.3 (Elizabethan); 823.4 (Later 17th Century); 823.5 (First half of 18th Century; Queen Anne, etc.); 823.6 (Later 18th Century to 1800); 823.7 (Early 19th Century to 1837); 823.8 (Victorian Fiction to 1900); 823.9 (20th Century); now usually sub-subdivided to 823.91 (Contemporary Fiction). By a suffix letter 'J' the same tables serve for Children's Fiction through the centuries. Follow the same procedure for German Fiction: 833; French: 843; Italian: 850; Spanish: 860; and so on, using the national number mnemonic as before, and period subdivisions to suit the national literature in question.

The third, and final feature is the building up of geographical and travel literature numbers, within the main class of 900, but separated from history and biography. Again, simplicity itself; and ingeniously contrived, requiring neither memory nor further study beyond the elements already grasped. You will remember that 940 is DC for Europe: History. You can make the number for Europe: Travel and Geography by simply inserting the digit '1' between the first two digits, evolving 914 (discarding the final 'o'). From this we are able to think immediately of all the Travel numbers, without further effort: 914.2 (Geography and Travel: Great Britain); 914.3 (of Germany); 914.4 (of France); 914.5 (of Italy); 914.6 (of

Spain); 914.7 (of Russia) . . . on to the end of the national tables, which for practical purposes is 997.21 (Pitcairn Island) – 919.721 (Geography and Travel – Pitcairn Island). Classes 998 and 999 are reserved for Arctic and Antarctic Regions, and as books on these subjects must be Exploration, Travel, Geography and Description, the numbers used are almost sure to be 919.8/9 until the future gives these regions a 'History'.

Such, then, is a bare outline of the DC, in all its practical simplicity. Yet the librarians of NATO countries once met in conference to discuss the practicability of 'devising a new and more flexible system of classification suited to the needs of modern libraries'. (*Liaison*: News-Sheet of the Library Association, August, 1963.) I doubt if anything likely to be a noticeable improvement on DC ever came from this enquiry; but we may be sure, the search for a better scheme will go on. Classification is a challenge; an education in itself; a fascinating mental exercise; and is sure to engage the active interest of future generations of bibliographers. Meanwhile, as book-trade users, we must help to encourage booksellers and others to spend a little time with DC, because it is the most widely-used bibliographic classification and, above all, is the scheme used in BNB.

The complete tables may be consulted in all public libraries, and British agents for DC will supply the standard editions. For example, the 17th edition[2] (used by the larger libraries), in two volumes with the Relative Index, is available from the enterprising bookseller and school supplier Don Gresswell (1972 price for the set £14); and there is also the Abbreviated 9th edition in one volume, used by many school libraries (price £4·75). Gresswell also publishes in Britain a most useful *Guide to the Use of Dewey Decimal Classification* (based on the use of DC in the Office of the Library of Congress); and an *Introduction to DC for British Schools* by Marjorie Chambers, (75p).

The last-named book is worth study by those who think of adopting the system for the orderly arrangement of office papers, bibliographies and subject book lists, back lists and allied trade material. Students who become interested in the

2. It is reported that from January 1971 Library of Congress will use DC numbers from the new and enlarged 18th edition. From the same date BNB will also use this edition in its five-year cumulation for 1971–1975.

subject beyond the requirements of the examination syllabus will find *Dewey Decimal Classification: an Appraisal* by J. Metcalfe (Clive Bingley, 1966) useful, and of course we must not overlook detailed study of its application in BNB and in public libraries, where it determines the arrangement of the book stock and of the subject catalogues.

Again, remember the *Oxford General Catalogue* mentioned above as an example of a great trade catalogue classified by DC, and also that Routledge's current catalogue (greatly improved in recent years) is now classified. Allen and Unwin's catalogue has already been mentioned.

The practice of denoting the DC number of technical books on the back of title-pages seems to have been largely discontinued since SBN became more widely applied, although one publisher does even use UDC for specialized scientific and technical monographs printed in Europe.

I will discuss later how useful such a practice can be in conveying to laymen precise information about the subject matter of books beyond the knowledge and sometimes the comprehension of all but the specialists in these scientific and technical subjects. Even to the people for whom such books are written and published the classification symbol conveys useful information as to the exact topic dealt with, and many booksellers are required to handle, select for stock, supply, and occasionally to report and recommend to customers books in their line.

A sign of the change which has taken place in the 1960's in respect of classification is also to be noticed in the classified order of the bookstock of at least one large shop. Others will follow in publishers' offices, bookshops, schools and offices.

QUESTIONS FOR RECAPITULATION

1. Write a brief statement showing your knowledge of the main classes of DC, and of the method of subdivision.

2. Describe the classified arrangement of the stock of your local library, and show how you find non-fiction books on a specific subject.

3. Write a concise statement on the application of DC to the

book trade, from publishers' catalogues to daily work in a shop.

4. What is meant by a 'form' of literature and a 'form division' of certain non-fiction books as used in DC?

5. Make a list of every trade publication, book list, cumulation, publisher's catalogue, index which you are conversant with, and in which the arrangement of entries is according to DC. Include American publications.

Chapter 8
'As Easy as ABC': a Note on Alphabetization

Here it will be useful to interpolate a brief statement about A–Z: that is, about alphabetization, which is often thought by the untrained indexer to be a simple matter: in fact, to be 'as easy as ABC'. Nothing could be more inaccurate, for alphabetization results only from a strict adherence to rules. Without this, inconsistencies occur, causing difficulties and exasperation when users of catalogues and indexes try to locate books and topics.

Thus it should be a first duty when beginning to use *British Books in Print* (or any other A–Z catalogue) to read all the prelims, which in this particular work are indeed headed: *How to Use British Books in Print*. Rules clearly set out in this statement should be memorized, special notes being made on the arrangement of entries, and the conventions followed when dealing with surnames with a prefix (Mac, Mc, M'); and the rule adopted with regard to hyphenated names. Here the editorial practice is to enter under the last part of a surname (V. Sackville-West appears under 'West, V. Sackville-') and 'for the sake of consistency' prefixes such as 'la', etc., have been treated similarly. This appears to many users (the present writer included) to be an unfortunate choice. A name is a name; Sheila Kaye-Smith's surname was Kaye-Smith, not Smith; and when we consider such names as Walter de la Mare we see that consistency has indeed served us badly, for who ever thinks of the poet as Mare? Yet one has to look for details of his many books under 'Mare, Walter de la'; although his own choice of name was 'de la Mare', for his family name was Delamare; however, we do find De Foe under Defoe, few writers now favouring the separation of prefix from true surname. It would seem that there is a sound case for all trade bibliographers, including publishers' catalogue editors, to be advised to consider adopting a recognized code for cataloguers, instead of each making arbitrary and individual rules. Some careful thinking has been done for over half a century on cataloguing problems connected with authors' names, especially in America, and 'for the sake of consistency' as well as for the elimination of possible errors and the speeding-up of search work, it would be a useful decision if the two great trade associations could persuade members to follow an established code. Failing that, to adapt or adopt one to suit their needs, and to follow it. Switching from *British Books in Print* consultation to, say, a check for current prices in Faber's stock catalogue, the user must mentally switch from 'Mare', to quite rightly, 'de la Mare'. Beginners are often puzzled; this is only one example among scores; but a simple decision would eliminate all the problems and difficulties. But more about this when we come to consider publishers' catalogues; meanwhile, what has been said will emphasize the need for care and attention to forewords and prefaces of all reference books in constant use.

Proceeding, the student will then learn that the *British Books in Print* entries are arranged on the 'Word-by-Word' system. Many will have used the book without having noticed this, or indeed, without having realized that there are two methods of dealing with the alphabetization of names and book titles.

When using the phrase, 'as easy as ABC', if we mean 'as easy as alphabetization' we make a misleading comparison, because the arrangement of a large number of names, especially of titles of books, in a strict alphabetical sequence according to one of the two systems, is not as easy as many students think. Try it. Hand somebody about a hundred title slips in disorder, asking them to put the slips into a strict alphabetical sequence, either following Whitaker's choice of the 'word-by-word' order, or the alternative, known sometimes as the 'follow through' method. It is a safe bet you will get your slips back with some errors.

Word-by-word order is established by considering each word separately; then throwing the entries into order of the first words; followed by a second sorting according to the second words; and so on, until the final sequence is arrived at. Now the 'follow through' method disregards individual words and arranges titles and other entries into one strict alphabet according to the spelling followed through, letter by letter. Briefly, in word-by-word order *Horse Under Water*, by Len Deighton precedes the *Horseman's Year*, edited by Dorian Williams; under the other method, *Horseman's Year* comes first because the sorter ignores the words and spells through; as 'm' in the alphabet precedes the 'u' of *Under* the correct order is immediately established. To fix the difference clearly in your mind, take down the title volume of *British Books in Print*: 1970. Open it at random: let us say at the word 'Church'. Then mentally re-arrange these entries, or some of them, by the 'follow through' method. You will see that, whereas in *Books in Print* titles beginning with 'Church' all come together, with the secondary order established by alphabetizing second words, then third words, and so on, to give a sequence 'Church in the Sun, Church in Wales, Church Life, Church Needlework, . . . Churches and Cathedrals, Churches, Care of . . .' your re-arrangement by 'follow through' will result in 'Church Furnishing, Church Heating, Churchill, Sir Winston, Church of India . . .' Notice the intrusion of 'Churchill' between 'Heating' and 'India'. I much prefer word-by-word order. It is certainly easier on the eyes and more logical, in that each word is a pattern easily caught by a glance. The other order requires closer scanning.

If you have to arrange a mixture of proper names, authors, titles of books, and subjects you will come across many instances where the first word is common to authors, titles, and subjects. Here, word-by-word order, when strictly followed, always gives precedence to authors, then to subjects, and finally to titles.

But from 1968 *British Books in Print* stated that, 'The inclusion of separate alphabets under the same word where it is used with different meanings has been discontinued in favour of one straight alphabet.'

Summarizing 'as easy as ABC' by way of a recapitulary example, I suggest an exercise: write out on slips the following titles:

Sandars Lectures: Cambridge series
San Francisco Disaster (Sutherland)
Sanderson, Robert (Walton)
Sand of the Desert (Macdonald)
Sandby Drawings (Oppé)
Sandals at the Mosque (Cragg)
Sand and Gravel Industry, The (Graham)
Sanders of the River (Wallace)
Sand, George: biographies of (Gribble; Maurois)

Sand and Foam (Gibran)
San Sebastian (Smith)

Remembering all the points we have discussed and explained, first arrange your eleven slips by word-by-word method; then by 'follow through', noting before you start that 'Sand, George' is here a subject entry, not a title. Unless your arrangements coincide with the order given at the end of this chapter try again, selecting some similar sequences from a title index.

Opinions differ about the relative merits of the two systems, but I would expect strong support from constant users of indexes for my own preference, Whitaker's word-by-word, which seems to me to be much easier to follow, because it eliminates an additional mental process. 'Follow through' requires more visual and mental examination to follow than its rival. It is clear that when applied to hundreds of thousands of titles, the method adopted will be an important decision, not a minor one, at least as far as users are concerned.

When new atlases with gazetteer-indexes are offered for subscription, they should always be tested to find out if the system adopted has been strictly followed. Buyers can rapidly make a sort of 'do-it-yourself' Consumers' Association check. If an index is inconsistently (that is, incorrectly) arranged, booksellers' buyers may help to improve the next edition by pointing out the faults to the publisher's representative, emphasizing that such defects are likely to prejudice informed customers against the book, especially librarian customers, who are trained and experienced in such routine matters.

QUESTIONS FOR RECAPITULATION

1. What system of alphabetization do you prefer for the arrangement of a catalogue and an index? Give reasons and examples.

2. Having arranged the eleven index slips suggested in this chapter, check your arrangement with the following example, according to the method you have adopted:

Word-by-Word	*Follow Through*
San Francisco Disaster	Sandals at the Mosque

San Sebastian
Sand, George: biographies
   of (subject)
Sand and Foam
Sand and Gravel
Sand of the Desert
Sandals at the Mosque
Sandars Lectures
Sandby Drawings
Sanders of the River
Sanderson, Robert (subject)

Sand and Foam
Sand and Gravel
Sandars Lectures
Sandby Drawings
Sanders of the River
Sanderson, Robert
Sand, George
Sand of the Desert
San Francisco Disaster
San Sebastian

3. State briefly the system of alphabetization used in the current edition of *British Books in Print*, noting in particular the treatment of hyphenated surnames and names with prefixes.

Chapter 9
The Public Library Service and the Bookseller

In the past the average bookseller refused to think rationally on the subject of the public book supply and service established in Great Britain in the mid-nineteenth century. Prejudice against, and even hatred of, our library service even now appears in trade papers and may occasionally be heard at trade meetings.

But since the great increase in the public expenditure on books and libraries became really noticeable in local budgets, and the effects of the Roberts Report were plainly seen in counties, cities and towns, a more friendly attitude has slowly developed. Now there is no longer any useful purpose in discussing these matters: the only possible fundamental changes in library development foreseeable in Britain are pay collections for current fiction: payment of fees for the borrowing of books; and participation in the provision of library-user fees for authors under a scheme giving legal sanction to the recognition of a Public Lending Right (PLR).

To booksellers one would say: if you have library business, keep it and promote it, for this side of your trade should increase for decades to come; if you do not serve library customers, cease wasting time on deploring the existence of public libraries, stop making wild, inaccurate statements about specialist library booksellers, try your utmost to get into this side of your business, late in the day though it is for newcomers.

All students must have some knowledge of the establishment and administration of public libraries if they are to proceed satisfactorily with their work for the BA diploma. The brief descriptive and explanatory observations that follow should help newcomers to understand the minimum requirements, to become acquainted with the special problems of library book supply if they seek work with one of the big library booksellers (there are about twenty who are said to have captured about

80 per cent of the present business),[1] and to grasp the essentials of the library licensing system at present governing the commission allowed on net books supplied.

In addition, all booksellers have to remember from time to time that their local public libraries, which as ratepayers they help to maintain, are a useful extra-mural source of bibliographical information. Libraries subscribe to services and buy expensive bibliographical material beyond the resources (and daily needs) of all but the aristocrats of the trade, but their user need not, should not, be restricted to librarians.

So away with folk ideas handed down from the 1850's and on to the realism of the 1970's, with the great open university public hungry for study and academic books; and the exciting provision of a British and Commonwealth library service unequalled in the world round the corner, and with the equally inspiring development of technical, university, school, industrial and service library provision which has been pursued in the English-speaking world since 1950.

In the 1960's for the first time the Ministry of Education became actively involved in public library affairs to the extent of appointing a Committee or 'Working Party' who reported to the Minister on such specific developments as *Inter-Library Co-operation in England and Wales*, and the even more important establishment of *Standards of Public Library Service* (both published in 1962). Advisers appointed by the Minister of Education in 1961 affirmed their belief in 'the importance of the public library as a great and developing national asset' (p. 45). They advocated the provision of 'specialized bibliographical tools' (p. 46). Here is a recommendation that should interest every reader of this book. They recommended that 'every library giving the basic library service should purchase annually at least 3,000 volumes of adult fiction in the English language' (p. 47). This was an annoying recommendation to some critics, who regard the provision of current fiction as outside the sphere of public libraries.

When the Report was published I heard a leading bookseller deplore the omission of a recommendation limiting the supply

1. 'Rather surprisingly it turned out that publishers' business with the twenty library suppliers chosen represents almost 80 per cent of the total amount of money spent on books by the public libraries.' 'PLR: a practical approach.' *The Author*, Autumn, 1970 (pp. 97–98).

of fiction to novels and short stories of literary importance. He thought that the provision of Westerns and thrillers in public libraries was contrary to the principles of the initiators of mid-nineteenth-century legislation. He could not agree that the purchase of light fiction, merely to entertain readers, was a necessary part of the function of modern libraries serving citizens of the affluent society, adding that if this principle were accepted, to be consistent, local authorities should be empowered to offer cinema programmes of Western and thriller films as an entertainment to ratepayers in search of relaxation. This rider seems to me to be based on far-fetched, immaterial, and unsound reasoning. Unless a critic objects to the supply of contemporary fiction as a whole, it is impracticable to suggest the elimination of certain classes because they merely entertain the reader.

All fiction is written to entertain. The eighty-two years that have made *Treasure Island* and the same author's *New Arabian Nights* major (or minor, according to standards) classic fiction, have not changed the function or the value, or the nature of these books: the stories were written as 'light fiction' to entertain readers in search of recreation by reading. 'Pastime reading', to use Dr E. A. Savage's phrase, may also have some educative qualities: that depends very much on the reader. I suppose no critic other than the odd person who would exclude all fiction from libraries would object to the purchase in the best available editions of many copies of Stevenson's books. If this is agreed, are we then to conclude that it is the business of a local authority to give film shows of *Treasure Island*, the adventure of *The Cream Tarts*, and *The Pavilion on the Links*? Because we add *Madame Bovary* to our public supply of novels, must we put on stage versions of Flaubert's masterpiece? Of course not. We are considering public libraries and their place in the community, and must not confuse their problems with those relating to entertainment in other media. If we do put on a stage show it is an entirely separate sphere of the activities of a local authority, under separate legislation. The one does not follow from the other. If we accept the recommendation of the Roberts' Working Party on the provision of adult fiction adequately representing books 'currently reviewed in the main general and literary periodicals' (para. 46, p. 17) then we must leave it to those locally responsible to their communities to select what they think is most suited to their local needs.

However, there is now a realistic appreciation of the function of libraries and, above all, of the bibliographical services the national libraries, and BNB render to all of us, including the book trade and the authors who keep it going.

Thus it was encouraging to read the detailed report of the findings of the National Libraries Committee in the *Bookseller* for 14th June and 20th September 1969. It was reported that some London booksellers do 'use the library [that is, the British Museum] to check bibliographical information'; and that 'booksellers were interested in the wider implications of bibliography and would favour the production of subject bibliographies'.

In the latter part of 1970, we read that the result of collaboration between BNB, the National Cash Register Co., and an American firm, has been a marvellous new process perfected for the production of a complete listing of *Books in English*, on the lines of the national bibliographies, but in microfilm to be read by means of a special apparatus.

In the book world today there are more changes in a single year than in a decade of the first half of the century. This must mean that for the remainder of this century all sections of the book trade, libraries of all types, commercial enterprises involving the use of documentation, and the world of formal education, will have to work closely together with a good deal of understanding and tolerance.

New legislation has followed the publication of the Roberts' Report. In addition alterations have been made in the structure of local government service, because these are necessary when local boundaries are remapped to comply with the London Government Act, 1963 and associated legislation concerned with county boundaries. A brief summary of the service which follows, describes the position as it was in 1970. It is not likely to be radically changed, and as candidates, when attempting to answer questions, display varying degrees of ignorance about the matter, it should be useful if I discuss the various types of library authority and their function and explain how a good modern public library is arranged. In spite of one's assumption that candidates would have some knowledge of their local public library service through their personal use of it either as regular readers or as occasional reference library visitors, it is unusual to have a satisfactory answer submitted on this topic.

At the top of the hierarchy are

The National Libraries

of which the British Museum is the greatest. The Library of the
BM is one of six 'copyright' libraries – so called because of
privileges accorded to them under the Copyright Acts of 1911
and 1956. The others are the Bodleian Library at Oxford,
named after its benefactor, Sir Thomas Bodley (1545–1613),
who greatly extended the university library founded by
Humphrey, Duke of Gloucester; the Cambridge University
Library; the National Library of Scotland; the National
Library of Wales; and Trinity College, Dublin. These 'Copyright Deposit' libraries are entitled to one copy of every new
book published in Great Britain, although in practice only the
BM library takes everything. It is the publisher's legal obligation
to deposit in the BM a copy of the best edition of every book he
publishes, this being done usually through the agency of a
central collecting office. The other national libraries apply for
the books they require, but the National Library of Wales is
not entitled to the full privileges of the system. It should be
remembered that these national libraries are all reference
libraries. In order to use the books they collect, scholars and
students must attend personally at the reading rooms and, where
available, the special departments, such as the King's Library
in the BM. Publishers look upon this 'privilege' as a burden
unjustly thrust upon them by tradition, and with the support of
a Royal Commission, whose report has so far lain dormant,
may soon try to obtain some relief by modification, if not complete abolition of the privilege, except its application to the BM.
Certainly its extension to the new university libraries now being
founded, as suggested in the national press, will be most
strongly resisted.

All students who work in London and the Home Counties
should try to visit the BM Reading Room at least once, to see
for themselves how this vast reference library serves research
workers, authors, scholars and teachers. The great name
catalogue (authors, academies, anonyma), with subject indexes,
is a superlatively well-edited tool. Its faults are due to the
colossal nature of the undertaking itself, and the impossibility
of finality. The photolithographic edition of this *General*

Catalogue of Printed Books, published between 1960 and 1966 in 263 volumes (13¾ × 9) with about 1,000 columns per volume, is a triumph of British scholarship and technical skill. It soon went out of print; but there is a marvellous Readers Compact Edition in 26 volumes (£268 the set). Bibliographers and scholars now have the greatest bibliographical aid to come from this country in the history of learning.

Subject to occasional restrictions due to alterations and re-decoration personal application at the office usually enables students to obtain a day ticket admitting them on one occasion to the Reading Room, where they will find thousands of standard reference works, including author, subject, and form bibliographies on the open shelves, the bibliographies being located for the most part in the small presses at the ends of the radial desks, which are the spokes in the vast wheel of the room, the hub being the superintendent's circular office and desk where the assistants and runners work.

Here too, since 1950, is located the card catalogue of additions to the library, 1950 to date, providing through the BNB catalogue cards service a speedy, up-to-date author and subject bibliography from the time of the formation of BNB.

There are other national libraries of a different type. The most famous of these is

The National Central Library

formerly the Central Library for Students, founded in 1916 by that great educator and initiator, Dr Albert Mansbridge, C.H. (1878–1952), to provide a lending service to adult students taking university extension courses, WEA lecture classes and similar extra-mural study courses. The importance of its work was eventually recognized by the Treasury, and this inspiring example of what can be achieved by a great man of vision, has had since 1931, when it became the NCL, the cost of its administration and service to the community paid for by a government grant, with continued financial help from the Carnegie United Kingdom Trust, the Rockefeller Foundation, and other benefactors.

In addition, public and other libraries using the NCL pay annual subscriptions through their local and other authorities. The stock of the NCL is non-fiction, largely acquired to meet the needs of students from matriculation level up to research and postgraduate studies. Adult classes usually require many copies of the same textbook to be used at the same period; to meet this demand would be burdensome and uneconomic for a public library. In practice it would be virtually impossible to render such a service from a town library. Moreover specialists usually require expensive monographs; sometimes rare or scarce books; and similar material. Even university and specialist libraries may not be able to meet this demand, but by the well-organized service of interlending through the NCL it is possible to obtain a very large proportion of all requests received in a normal year's working. I remember obtaining soon after the foundation of the NCL a copy of a scarce treatise in German (never translated), for a local doctor who was writing a monograph. No copy could be located in any library in Great Britain. So the NCL went outside the country for one, and in due course a German specialist or learned library posted a copy to the NCL, who forwarded it on extended loan for study in the suburban library from which we had made the application on behalf of the doctor. This type of service is now normal routine, and on this scale may be unique in the world of librarianship. Critics of the library services usually overlook these developments, which have evolved quietly and without ballyhoo, simply because of the energies of goodwill and the inspiration of Dr Albert Mansbridge, whose work as an educator must never be forgotten.

Requests for books are met by NCL not only from their own stock of books and from public libraries co-operating in the interlending system, but also from certain specialist collections, semi-private collections, and institutional libraries enrolled as 'Outliers'. One example will suffice: the great library of the British Drama League, the largest of its kind in the Commonwealth, and one of the largest in the world of the theatre, is an Outlier Library.

County and Municipal Libraries

Enough has been described relating to this truly remarkable service to provide the bookseller student with material to answer questions on libraries except the ordinary public libraries. Briefly, the public library service of Great Britain, as it has

6

developed since the Public Libraries Act of 1919, comprises a service through County Libraries to villages, districts and towns where the Act had not been locally adopted. Next to the County Libraries come those maintained by county boroughs, boroughs (including the metropolitan boroughs, the City of London, and the City of Westminster), and the urban districts. Most of these were established between 1850 and 1892: 1893 and 1919 (the parliamentary milestones in library legislation). If a municipal council had not adopted the Acts before 1919, thereafter it came automatically under the county council for its library service, unless permission to contract out could be obtained from the higher authority.

In counties the librarian is an executive and administrative official under the county education officer, and the library committee is often a sub-committee, with delegated powers subject to report. In municipal boroughs and urban districts the town council elects a libraries committee, appoints a borough or chief librarian responsible to his committee, and to the town council. The modern service comprises a lending department for adults; a children's or junior library, usually in the charge of a woman specially trained for work with young readers; a reference library and information department under a special staff; with branch libraries and delivery service points, including mobile libraries operating in towns with new estates situated more than three miles from the nearest library building. County libraries consist of a headquarters administrative unit, sometimes located, as at Hertford, in the county hall, sometimes in separate, specially-built premises, together with a series of regional or district libraries and branches, and even village centres, in order to provide a full service, linked with headquarters, throughout the county area. I do not think there is any other country in the world, not even the United States of America, where the library coverage is geographically so near to perfection.

Out of the formation of regional interlending bureaux and systems, promoted by the present writer in 1927, has developed union catalogues, and close co-operation between libraries, with NCL, as we have seen, as the focus and the great central information office for bibliographical co-ordination. My paper read to a conference of special librarians at Trinity College, Cambridge, in September 1927, advocated the formation of a union catalogue of the reference libraries of the twenty-eight metropolitan borough libraries, to facilitate interlending. It attracted the attention of the Secretary of the Carnegie United Kingdom Trust. Within a few months a committee had been formed, the Trust had financed the project, and work had begun on the giant catalogue, housed at NCL, the largest of its kind in the country until the formation of BNB in 1950. The movement soon spread to all regions, many of them improving on our initial scheme by the elimination of a union catalogue.

Regional Library Bureaux are now firmly established in the British library landscape. From the time of their inception those responsible planned for developments. I will mention here one only, selected because it concerns booksellers who are library suppliers. This is

Subject Specialization

whereby libraries within a region have allocated to them blocks of Dewey class numbers covering in the aggregate, within the region, the whole of the Dewey tables. Libraries in the scheme undertake to buy every new book published on the subjects allocated to them, up to a limit of £6 for a single volume. Above that they may be selective. Thus within the region all new non-fiction books except trivia are bought, week by week. An index to subject specializing libraries quickly informs specialists where new books on their own subjects are collected. These books are freely interloaned. Now many library suppliers using BNB undertake to send books required under this scheme to their library customers by weekly routine, without the clerical work involved in sending orders to booksellers. Such booksellers check BNB every week against the class lists supplied by libraries, and automatically supply the required items.

Library trade is well worth pursuing, for apart from its effect on the economics of bookselling and publishing there is the value to the staff of regularly handling orders for technical and the older standard books which might not normally be stocked. Book knowledge thus acquired equips an assistant for life.

Public Library expenditure on books has risen from under £7 million in 1964/5 (with 420 authorities), to an estimated £11,150,000 (from 367 authorities) in 1968/9.

We truly can now regard our libraries as a vast bookshop

window for books old and new, advertising our books for the Trade and bringing them to the notice of potential buyers. We welcome the help public librarians render the cause of books in general, by educating readers, training literary taste, creating new readers, helping young people to regard books as an essential part of the life of a civilized member of the community, arranging lectures on books, reading and authors, promoting exhibitions of good books for children, books for presents, and books on specific subjects, and even issuing printed publicity of books and reading, which in some city and larger town libraries is considerable in quantity and high in quality.

Yet in 1963 one of the most distinguished and successful London booksellers was reported in *Books* to be in agreement with the interviewer who said 'one of the two chief factors that restrict the sale of books are public libraries'. Some such remark has been heard so often that one is inclined to believe the cynics who allege that we believe what we want to believe, seldom forming our opinions on things as they are even if the facts are easily ascertainable.

Nothing has been said in this chapter about school libraries, nor about the technical libraries maintained by great scientific and industrial firms, such as ICI, Kodak, the Metal Box Company; nor of the large libraries connected with professional and technical institutes, such as the Institution of Electrical Engineers, the Cambridge Institute of Criminology, the Institute of Bankers; nor of the specialist libraries of academic societies, such as the Historical Association; nor of the National Lending Library of Science and Technology, at Boston Spa, Yorkshire. They all form part of the pattern of the library resources of the country, and, as sources of special information, will be alluded to in a later chapter. Many of them subscribe to the association known as ASLIB, concerned with the retrieval of scientific and technical information, documentation, the bibliography of current technical and scientific literature, abstracts, and related material, all of which is the very lifeblood of a modern society depending on industrial and scientific research.

Those who are employed in retail shops which do serve libraries should, indeed must, be familiar with the NBA and that section of it usually referred to as the 'Library Agreement', which originally came into force on 12th November 1929, and since that date has governed the supply of net books to libraries. The three signatories represented the Publishers Association, the Booksellers Association and the Library Association. A second Memorandum with minor amendments came into force 1st May 1933. In 1963 the Library Association gave notice of its intention to withdraw from the Agreement, leaving it to the two trade associations to draw up and enforce a new one. This may extend the permission granted to library authorities to 'receive from and at the expense of a named bookseller or booksellers a COMMISSION on new books . . .' (quoted from the Memorandum, as set out in *Book Trade Organisation*, edited by F. D. Sanders, Allen and Unwin, 1939), to school libraries, and may even vary the commission of 'not exceeding ten per centum of the value of such purchases for prompt payment'. In practice the full 10 per cent is given to all library orders for new books, and alas, in practice, payment is often far from prompt. For further details refer to Appendix 3.

Library orders in general do provide all the bibliographical details required by booksellers, who, because of the 10 per cent discount they must offer, do not expect to have to search for publishers and prices. Nevertheless orders are often troublesome, especially when they include a large number of books 'on approval', items published by societies, local printers, private publishers, authors' own printings, pamphlets, booklets, and similar fugitive material never subscribed to the trade, and for which trade terms are not available. These items are supplied at a loss to the bookseller, who is willing and able to obtain them only if he receives a fair share of the library's business.

Next to prompt service, booksellers must make sure that books that cannot be supplied are noted by routine, and the 'answers' from Book Centre and publishers' trade counters forwarded at once to the library office responsible for the buying administration. Failure to do this will usually result in dwindling orders and perhaps to a request for the bookseller's name to be deleted from the library licence, which in some amended form will certainly be retained under any revision of the scheme.

Perhaps the most difficult side of library supply business is the 'servicing' of books, although for the local bookseller the 'on approval' demands made by many librarians run it close. I have seen orders marked 'on appro' which have included books that could be supplied only to order (o/t/o) from USA, and remote European countries. But more often than not this unreasonable demand is amended after a friendly discussion between the librarian and the retailer. The servicing of library books includes the supply and fitting of a plastic sleeve, and may extend to the affixing of board labels, the typing of index or catalogue cards, the supply and writing of a book card, rubber stamping, and so on. This is one of the most difficult problems in the trade, because as stated in the NBA Judgment, 'It is not possible to cost these services with absolutely demonstrable accuracy. . . .' 'Competition is keen, and there is variety in the amounts charged for services' (see *Bookseller*, 3rd November 1962, p. 1842). Whatever the outcome of discussions on the topic, the local bookseller is seldom able to compete with the specialist bookseller in this particular side of library business. Many librarians are sympathetic enough not to expect the same degree of service required from the specialist, limiting demands to the supply and fitting of the plastic sleeve, at cost, plus a small allowance for profit.

This degree of understanding and co-operation must vary considerably, and as we learnt from the evidence submitted in Court, can range from complete indifference to and disregard of the problems inherent in keeping local bookshops open, to frankly expressed concern for the trading difficulties of booksellers in postwar Britain.

In an article entitled *The College Librarian and the Bookseller*, Mr Denison Smith, Librarian of Oxford College of Technology, discusses many new aspects of library business connected with the library supply to such specialist institutions as his own. The topic will undoubtedly receive a great deal of discussion in the next decade of this rapidly-changing era. Meanwhile, students may remember for the purposes of the examination that at least in one respect, this technical librarian's hope that close co-operation will be developed is already realized in numerous counties and towns. 'Is it inconceivable that one day,' he asks, 'surmounting the obstacles of local government service and private enterprise, there might be co-operation in the provision of the less obvious bibliographies and catalogues, not only among libraries, but also between libraries and local booksellers, so that, between them, they can trace virtually everything, each sometimes calling on the other for assistance?' (*Bookseller*, 10th August 1963, p. 1018.) Such co-operation does exist; it will be encouraged; it must be remembered both in daily work and in the examination hall.

Detailed discussion and analysis of all problems connected with library book supply will be found in *Library Bookselling*, by F. T. Bell and the present writer, published in 1966 by André Deutsch in the *Grafton Books* series. Interested students and specialist booksellers are referred to this and to *Books and Libraries*, by R. O. Linden, Cassell, 1965.

RECAPITULATION

1. Questions are usually limited to those testing candidates' knowledge of the arrangement of public libraries; the type of catalogues used; the classification scheme; and the adaptation to the layout and display of bookshops.

2. Advanced students will also be able to give specific examples of the bibliographical range and services of large library systems, and the manner in which booksellers can take advantage of this in dealing with certain types of orders from specialist customers.

3. Changes in the Library Agreement and allied matters may attract more detailed questions on these topics, as discussed in this chapter, and in *Library Bookselling*.

Chapter 10
Publishers' Catalogues and the Terminology of Bibliography

Except in communist countries publishing is the most individual industry surviving today. State control in totalitarian regimes imposes uniformity, but in Britain and in other countries the freedom of choice and the infinite variety of publishers' catalogues is so important that all of us in the book trade would resist any attempt to force publishers to conform to a pattern, either in production or style of presentation.

Personalities of the world of publishing are reflected in the kind of books published, style of publicity and catalogues, both seasonal and general. So much so that experienced bookmen recognize the characteristics which distinguish the books of certain firms, even before they glance at the imprint. They will recognize a Cape book, distinguish a Faber volume from its shelf companions, as quickly as an art dealer will recognize a Derain or a Peter De Wint. I once knew a bookseller who could name correctly the publishers of four out of six different volumes handed to him to feel in the dark.

This is all to the good, and a tribute to the personal style of notable firms. But it must not preclude an acknowledgment of the great advantages for everybody of a certain degree of standardization in the presentation of the general catalogue of every large publishing house. These catalogues are advertisements for the publishers and their authors, and I regard them as the most important of all forms of publicity.

Back lists vary as much as the faces of their firms' publicity managers, and to ask for uniformity would be undesirable as well as a waste of time. Nevertheless the Publishers Association has recently shown signs of the need for some standards to be adopted. For example, it is now uncommon to come across an undated book. Some critics want more. A leading article in the *Times Literary Supplement*, 5th April 1963, p. 233, headed *Informative Publishing* suggests that very few publishers take the trouble to print detailed bibliographical information on the reverse of title pages. The writer asks for 'exact details of the work's previous publication . . . some indication of whether an original text had been corrected, re-written . . . or in any other way altered'. He even wants 'the size of the edition (as in several continental countries)', concluding 'it seems odd that there should be no kind of agreement or convention among British publishers about the information they should give'.

A discussion of these points would be out of place here, but I do wish very strongly to ask those with influence to go on striving for some 'kind of agreement or convention' in the matter of complete catalogues. Let there be as much variety in these as far as style is concerned as there is in seasonal lists, special lists and extra publicity material, but every publisher with a back list worth advertising should conform to a reasonable standard of cataloguing and presentation.

This topic gets an airing from time to time in the trade press. Reference to the files of the *Bookseller* will reveal detailed examination of named publishers' catalogues by the present writer. This was a decade ago, and improvements resulted, but one hopes for more. The *Bookseller* dated 25th July 1970 is worth consulting for its reference to a 1966 report on a standard entitled *Essentials in Catalogue Content and Format* arising from a discussion initiated by the Publishers Publicity Circle. This specifically concerned a scheme for combined seasonal catalogues (standard six-monthly announcements). We now have a subject guide to forthcoming books appearing six times a year.

Authors are beginning to realize that bad cataloguing by their publishers will bury details of their books, hinder sales, and in extreme cases prevent customers from buying. It is not always the fault of the bookseller that inaccurate, often exasperatingly wrong information should be given to potential customers. Bad catalogues encourage bad service, for booksellers have to use the catalogues of hundreds of firms, often in the hurried daily work of a busy shop, not in the quietude of an office. Moreover, assistants must vary in their personal knowledge, training and experience.

To be efficient tools under these circumstances catalogues must yield bibliographical information quickly, and should not be compiled haphazardly and carelessly. Authors too, are badly served if their books are not properly listed and indexed. At a meeting of PEN Club some years ago I gave many specific examples of the way in which defects in substandard catalogues could hinder sales. Title indexes contain entries under the wrong part of the title; author indexes frequently have entries for some edited books under the name of the editors only, ignoring completely the authors. Compilers do not understand that the author of a volume of letters is the person who wrote the letters, nearly always a well-known person, whose name we remember, while we do not remember the editor. Hence a busy or inexperienced assistant sometimes erroneously informs a customer that a particular book is now o.p., because 'it is no longer in the publisher's catalogue'. I once told a telephoning enquirer that a scholarly edition of John Donne's *Songs and Sonets* was apparently o.p.; the book was in fact available, but it was indexed under the editor's name, and not the author's, in an index of authors.

Publishers' cataloguers are frequently unaware of the correct part of an author's name to index: German surnames will be alphabetized under the prefix 'Von'; French names under 'De'; La Rochefoucauld was for some years in a university publishers' list under Rochefoucauld, not under the definite article, with no cross-reference to minimize the error; and one is never quite sure if La Fontaine will be found, first try, under 'La'; illustrators may be indexed, but not the authors of the books they have drawn pictures for. Happily, marked improvements have been noticed lately. One would like the PA to persuade members, without surrendering individuality, to conform now to an agreed standard. Publishers work only with one catalogue – their own; trade counter assistants usually know their lists by heart, and have no difficulty in finding their quick way through the one catalogue they handle. But booksellers work with hundreds, using them every hour of the day.

Seasonal lists and advance announcements do not matter so much, but even here there is a bare minimum not always achieved. I once received a stencilled advance list extending to four (unnumbered) quarto pages, and deduced the name of the publisher of the advertised new books by noting an addition to his well-known series; one had to guess, because the list lacked a heading with the publisher's name. Again, even a few well-printed and well-produced catalogues still hide the publisher's imprint: one has to look for it inside the front cover.

After even these few examples, it will perhaps be agreed that the trade must eventually adhere to a cataloguing code. Already we have a code for *Bibliographical References* published by British Standards Institution, and until the general code we have in mind is compiled and officially adopted, the best guide for those working in publishers' offices who are given the task of preparing the general list is a first-class catalogue from a great firm which may be used as a model.

In doubt as to the correct, or best, part of an author's name to index, they could, no, should, consult a standard reference book as a guide, instead of chancing it so erratically: Chambers's excellent *Biographical Dictionary*, for example, is exemplary as a guide for many difficult names; and the *Oxford Companion to French Literature* is authoritative in the treatment of French surnames.

Once again, the importance of the public library must be stressed, for it should be remembered that it is part of the training of the qualified librarian to learn how to catalogue according to a well-established, widely-followed, code of rules. Our thinking has been done for us. Why ignore it? And BNB can always be relied upon: their standard is a model of perfection; so is the cataloguing of CBI. But cataloguing is improving. A famous firm recently enlisted the help of a public librarian in remodelling a complete catalogue. Others might well do the same.

Of all British book catalogues, the *Oxford University Press General Catalogue* is supreme. All publishers, with the exception of a score, might well take a new look at their catalogues, measuring them against the best examples in the trade. Their own interests, those of their authors, and certainly those of the retail trade, would benefit by the scrutiny.

Terminology

Students working solely with an eye on the examination need not bother much with the terminology of bibliography. But a certain type of question can be answered more fully if candidates are familiar with the meanings of terms, especially those frequently used in publishers' catalogues, blurbs, and the reviews of critics in the weeklies. Here then is a subject worth some attention from average students, who may be asked as a preliminary, to spend twenty minutes with the *Oxford University*

Press General Catalogue mentioned above, and thus check their understanding of, for example, the description under *Oxford English Texts*: '. . . the texts constituted by *critical recension* of the original printings *collated* with such MSS as are extant . . .' (my italics). From such students and others, I would ask for agreement with my firmly held opinion, that all who work with books, and earn their living by publishing and selling them, should know what authors and their publishers mean when they describe certain books as 'definitive editions'; refer to 'redactions'; issue what are known as 'Variorum Editions'. True, many terms are misused, and I will give some examples of this later, but foreign and institutional customers frequently ask for advice before buying what they hope will be the best editions for their particular needs. This frequently occurs with certain classics (*Gulliver's Travels*; Darwin's *Origin of Species*, for example). They rightly expect their booksellers to know the meaning of terms they use when placing orders. Therefore the remainder of this chapter will be devoted to a 'bookseller's glossary' defining and annotating in detail the principal terms used in the editing and preparation of books; cited by the publishers of learned, academic and scholarly books, by bibliographers preparing publicity for standard books in new editions, and occasionally by customers with a collector's or specialist's knowledge.

Glossary with examples:

Acronym: a made-up word from the initial letters of a number of words. Example: radar, Nato.

Apparatus Criticus: sources of information, materials for textual study, manuscripts, letters and other material, relating to documents, MSS, and books, presented by an editor, usually in the form of footnotes, marginalia, and commentary, in support of his text, and thus associated with the preparation of a definitive edition of an author's work, especially where variant readings, doubtful texts, and obscurities occur. See also *Definitive Edition.* Example: *The Collected Poems of Wilfred Owen,* edited with an introduction and notes by C. Day Lewis, Chatto and Windus, 1963. 'The purpose of the notes is not to give a complete *apparatus criticus,* but chiefly to record such variants as show how Owen improved a line or passage . . . or variants which are of intrinsic interest.' See also *Editor's introduction.* Example: Dr J. Dover Wilson's introduction to his text of *Hamlet* (New Cambridge Shakespeare).

Catalogue Raisonné: an annotated list of an author's works, especially an artist's pictures, engravings, etc. (for example, the works of William Blake), with editorial commentary. Items in the catalogue are systematically arranged, sometimes in classified groups. Example: *Fra Angelico*, by John Pope-Hennessy: a complete edition, with 133 plates, 7 colour plates, 90 pages introduction, catalogue raisonné, 65 text illustrations, Phaidon Press, 1952.

Classic: So loosely used now that it is beginning to lack precise meaning, but still retaining its original associations with the literature of Greek and Latin authors and with the great, or standard works of permanent value, in later world literature. Briefly, a classic work, whether it is a monograph on some medical topic, or a novel by Emily Brontë, or a masterpiece in French dramatic literature, should be of the kind that by common consent will always be important and attract readers from every generation. *The Classics in Translation*, by F. Seymour Smith, Charles Scribner's, 1930, o.p., is an annotated bibliography of the Greek and Latin classics translated into English. Examples: books in series, such as *Everyman's Library* and many books in *World's Classics*, Dent's *Children's Illustrated Classics* and *Classics in Science.*

Collation in its technical, bibliographical meaning, refers to (a) that part of a cataloguing entry describing a book in its make-up, i.e. the book as a physical object: hence, it enumerates, as applicable to each individual book, the following features: number of volumes (if more than one); pagination, e.g. viii, 496 pp. indicates the prelims. or preliminary matter and the body of the work; illustrations, plates, whether in colour or otherwise, text drawings, facsimiles, diagrams; bibliography (usually abbreviated to bib., and to be noted as a source of information for those compiling booklists); size (often in centimetres); binding, if noteworthy, as e.g. half-leather, paper covers, boards, limp covers, sewed; series, if any;

sometimes contents note. Example: any entry in BNB; for instance, the model entry given in the preface to an annual cumulation; and (b) the term also means, in bibliography, the detailed comparison of manuscripts, documents, texts in printed form, in order to establish a definitive or standard text. One copy of a book may be compared by an expert in first editions with another, in order to ascertain which *is* the first edition. In the bookbinding trade, collation is a term used to describe the work of making sure that the sheets, as printed, have been arranged in their correct order. See also *Signature.* Comparison for verification, requiring the description enumerated above, is the process. The term has an interesting history, showing the ingenious development of the word from medieval times, when in certain monasteries, comparative readings, followed by debates, were made from the writings of the Christian Fathers (see also *Patristics*) hence, *Collationes patrum,* usually followed by a light repast, gave the word a modern meaning associated with weddings, cold collations, and so forth.

Colophon formerly referred to the ornamental 'tail-piece' at the end of a book, the word being derived from the Greek *kolophon,* meaning 'summit'. In addition to the printer-publisher's ornament, which of course serves as an identification symbol in the collection of old books by antiquarian dealers and collectors, information was usually printed here about the name of the printer, where printed, date of publication. Thus to a cataloguer the colophon section of his entry refers to the *Imprint* (see below). The word now means a publisher's device. Examples: the Bull colophon on Hutchinson's books and catalogues; Heinemann's Windmill; the Fox of Hart-Davis, and its association with the *Reynard* series; and the Dolphins in a medallion which distinguish Thames and Hudson's publications. Refer also to the *Bookseller* dated 22nd May 1971 for an illustration of ten ABP colophons redesigned.

Concordance is a term first used by Alexander Cruden (1701–1770) to entitle his dictionary of the Bible, with a citation, or 'agreement' of passages. Since 1737 concordance has been used by many other compilers for their literary dictionaries.

Critical Edition refers to a scholarly text, established by an editor after original research, collation of manuscripts, etc. Such an edition is characterized by the *apparatus criticus* submitted in the form of introduction, notes and commentary, to justify the text. The editorial work is therefore often considerable, especially in textural criticism, the elucidation of a crux, or problem presenting difficulties of interpretation. Examples: *Poems of Sir Philip Sidney*, edited by William A. Ringler, OUP, 1962, a superb piece of work; and Sir Herbert Grierson's text of the *Poems of John Donne*, 2 vols., 1912, in the *Oxford Standard Series*. As no holograph manuscript sources are extant for Sidney and Donne, editors in their search for a definitive text of the poetical works are presented with many problems.

Crux is a scholar's term for a puzzling, difficult, and often unsolved problem in textual interpretation.

Definitive Edition is one offered by editor and publisher as a text unlikely ever to be superseded. It is the result of research, collation and interpretation, and the editor's purpose is to provide a text as close to his author's final intentions as is possible. Such an edition is characterized by its editorial introduction and notes, usually with *critical apparatus* varying according to the nature of the problems to be solved. A definitive text of Shakespeare's plays is virtually impossible. Hence we have a famous *Variorum* Shakespeare (see below under *Variorum Edition*). Examples: the *Poetical Works of John Keats* edited by H. W. Garrod; *Reminiscences of the English Lake Poets* (1834) by Thomas De Quincey, edited for the *Everyman Library* edition by Professor J. E. Jordan, 1961. Occasionally material does turn up after the publication of a definitive edition which makes it necessary to revise a former editor's textual decisions. For example, the cache of Boswell papers at Malahide Castle, when fully collated may suggest a few revisions and amendments even to the great edition of Boswell's *Life of Samuel Johnson*, 6 vols., edited by Birkbeck Hill (1887), revised by L. F. Powell, 1934–1950, for OUP. In passing, this may be referred to as an outstanding example of a classic and an edition offering *critical apparatus* on the grand scale.

Diatessaron: see under *Harmony, A.*

Editio Princeps is a bibliographer's term for the first printed edition of a book or work.

   Example: *Travels into Several Remote Nations of the World,* in Four Parts. By Lemuel Gulliver, First a Surgeon, and then a Captain of Several Ships. Vol. 1. London: Printed for Benj. Motte, 1726. (Copied from the entry in CBEL, vol. 2, p. 589.)

Fascicle is a term used to describe the separate publication of a chapter or section of a long book which the publisher intends to issue in instalments. Examples: The *Cambridge Ancient History:* which CUP advertised would be ('to prevent delay in the publication of a revised edition') issued separately in paperbound fascicles, normally consisting of one chapter; and *A Short-Title Catalogue of French Books, 1601–1700 in the Library of the British Museum* . . . which was published in fascicles over a period of about two years.

Gloss: a marginal or textual insertion made by an editor to explain a crux, or to provide students with an elucidatory comment, and to offer an interpretation of an obscure passage. Hence a *Glossary* is a collection or list of glosses, often of archaic and obsolete words. In modern books the term is used for the list of technical and specialized terms appended to a scientific work.

Handbook (or *Manual*): should be restricted to the type of book in the technical, medical and scientific classes which is written primarily for practitioners. Systematic treatment of a subject is here intended for those who have already pursued a course of study in it and who wish to have a handbook or manual by them for revision and reference. An example (of correct use) is A. Derek Farr's *A Laboratory Handbook of Blood Transfusion Techniques,* Heinemann, 1961, a practical handbook for use by the trained staff of a blood transfusion service or by students who intend to specialize in this branch of medicine. The term should not be used for the popular presentation of a scientific subject.

Harmony: a harmony is defined as 'a collection of parallel narratives'. See also under *Collation*, and *Parallel*, and for the specific application of the term see *The Holy Scriptures* in chapter 13 (pp. 138-142).

Holograph: refers to a document, such as the manuscript of a book, or a single poem, or a letter, written wholly in the handwriting of the author. Antiquarian collectors use the abbreviation ALS for 'autograph letter signed'. An example of a holograph recently acquired by the Trustees of the British Museum was the only known manuscript of Coleridge's *Kubla Khan*. This manuscript, which was not discovered until 1934, contains interesting variants from the published version of 1816.

Thus students here have an illustration of a variant reading in relation to a definitive text.

Imprint is the information now supplied by publishers on title pages (or on the back of title pages): namely, the publisher, the place of publication and the date. These details were formerly enclosed in a stamp impressed on documents: hence the origin of the term. In British cataloguing practice when the place of publication is London this is sometimes omitted. But BNB entries always include London, and add the published price.

Incunabula: books printed before the year 1501; literally, cradle books.

Introduction: author's term for a preliminary study of a subject. Allied to this is the old-fashioned term *Primer,* now usually found only in school textbooks. Of course, an 'Introduction' may often be a most advanced text, beyond the comprehension of non-specialists. Much depends on the subject matter. Example: *An Introduction to Immunochemical Specificity,* by W. C. Boyd, Interscience, 1962. But note also the use of this term for a popular *Introduction to Money,* by Honor Croome, Methuen, 1962. Thus it is not wise to trust to titles without examination of the books or publishers' descriptive notes.

Lexicon: a dictionary (sometimes a word-book). From seventeenth-century usage usually now used only for dictionaries of ancient languages, such as Greek, Syriac, Hebrew and Arabic.

7

Library Edition: publishers' term for an edition in hardcovers of a book also available in different format, often in a paperback edition or pocket-size volume. Example: Michael Greener's *Dictionary of Commerce*, originally a Penguin book, and later issued in an octavo, hardcover library edition by A. and C. Black, 1970.

Monograph is a book dealing with one topic, or one aspect of a larger subject, or on one person. One could cite a handbook on biochemistry, as an example of a general treatment of the subject for biochemists, and a monograph on vitamins and hormones. Series examples: *Atomic Structure and Chemical Bonding*, by F. Seel, Methuen (Monographs on Chemical Subjects), and *The North American Sabre*, by Ray Wagner, Macdonald (Aircraft Monographs).

Outline usually indicates popular treatment of a great subject, largely influenced by the most famous outline ever prepared for the general reader, namely *The Outline of History*, by H. G. Wells, Cassell, 1920, revised from time to time by Raymond Postgate. Note also that Bouquet's *Comparative Religion*, a popular Penguin, is described by its author as 'A Short Outline'.

Parallel Text is used to denote to booksellers and customers that two different versions of the same work, or the original text and a translation into English or another language, are given. For example, a poem or a story in French, or a piece of prose in Latin, is printed *recto*, and the translation of the same passage is given *verso*. Examples: *Loeb Classical Library*, published by Heinemann, and in USA by Harvard University Press; being a unique, comprehensive and uniform series of classical Greek and Latin texts, with parallel English translations. Every student should know this magnificent series, founded by Dr James Loeb, because it is one of the most distinguished series in twentieth-century publishing, and when complete will consist of 450 titles, containing all that is worth reading in Greek and Latin literature from Homer to the end of the Western Empire. Each volume now costs (1972) £1·50 but it must be pointed out that as it is a parallel text edition, the customer is getting two books in one. The other example I wish to cite is of a different sort. When Wordsworth first wrote his autobiographical poem called *The Prelude; or, Growth of a Poet's Mind*, he conceived it as one of a series, to include not only this poem, but also *The Excursion* (1814). But he did not complete his project, and *The Prelude*, although read by his circle, remained in manuscript unpublished. Through his long life he revised, sometimes rewrote, certain passages, the alterations being of considerable interest to posterity, as they reveal developments in the poet's craft and use of words, and to biographers and critics, sometimes indicated changes of thought and opinion. Hence the importance of the parallel text edition of this classic in *Oxford English Texts*, edited by Ernest de Selincourt, OUP, 1926, revised by Helen Darbishire, 1959. These two devoted and supreme Wordsworthian scholars edited the poem from a collation of all extant manuscripts, and in the OET edition give students the 1805–6 version, the revisions of 1817–19; parallel with the 1850 posthumously published version. This great edition is therefore another example of a definitive one, providing *apparatus criticus*, introduction, and notes. This is the scholar's edition to recommend; but note that only the 1805 text is given separately in the *Oxford Standard Authors* edition. If customers want the 1850 text, give them volume three of the *Everyman* Wordsworth which also contains *The Excursion,* and *The Recluse,* to which the greater poem was intended as 'The Prelude'.

To complete the subject, note also *Harrap's Bilingual Series* containing books in French, German, Italian, Russian, Spanish, and Swedish, with the original text and the English translation parallel, intended for language students; and *Nelson's Mediaeval Texts*, a learned series of Latin Chronicles and other works including the lives of medieval saints (St Hugh of Lincoln) written by monks, and here presented in parallel text, with translations into modern English.

Patristics is a series term denoting books on the writings of the Fathers of the Christian Church. Examples: *The Library of Christian Classics*, edited by John Baillie and others, SCM, 1953– in progress, and, *Ancient Christian Writers* series, Longman, 1946– in progress. There is also a handy selection from the writings of the Fathers, edited and translated by Henry Bettenson, OUP, 1956.

Plain Text: a frequent request from teachers and students. It describes an edition of a classic, intended for study in class or with a tutor, which provides no notes, and perhaps not even an introduction, thus helping the student to work on the poem or essay direct, and encouraging his own critical judgment. Example: Byron's *The Vision of Judgement*, CUP (Cambridge Plain Texts), 1926, 48 pp.

Recension from *recensio*, denoting a reviewing or a revision. 'The choice between extant readings is the work of *recensio*', writes J. C. Maxwell in Cassell's *Encyclopaedia of Literature*, vol. 1, p. 543. Used in describing the characteristics of scholarly editions, such as those in *Oxford English Texts*, in which existing texts are thoroughly re-edited, revised, and re-examined by collation with all known sources of textual emendation. Example: a perfect one provided by the most important addition to *Everyman* for many years, namely, *Shakespearean Criticism*, by S. T. Coleridge, edited by Professor T. M. Raysor, 2 vols. Dent, EML, 162/183, 1961. Professor Raysor's original edition of 1930 was the standard text of this difficult work (see *Redaction* below, for reason), but, states *Everyman*, the series edition is 'essentially a recension of the well-known Raysor text . . . to bring the work into line with the latest Coleridge research'. (Quoted from *The Reader's Guide to Everyman's Library*, by A. J. Hoppé, Dent, 1962, p. 78.) See also *Apparatus Criticus*.

Recto is a bibliographer's and cataloguer's term for the right-hand side of a page of an open book; *verso* is the left-hand side of that page, to be read second to *recto*. Associated loosely with *Parallel Text*, which see above.

Redaction is a French term (rédacteur – editor; rédaction – the work of editing) now adopted into English to describe a special kind of editing; that which requires the arrangement and collation of manuscript material, left in a state, or handed over by the author in a state, unsuitable for publication. A redaction, therefore, indicates considerable editorial labour, and is frequently required before diaries or journals, personal narratives, and similar material are ready for publication. Sometimes a redaction will make it possible to publish important work which was left at an author's death merely in the form of notes. Example: Coleridge's *Shakespearean Lectures* were not written out in full, but had to be in part reconstructed from notes, fugitive material, etc. Sara Coleridge edited them from notes for her first, posthumous edition of 1849. See under *Recension*, above, for details of Raysor's two important editions. Pascal's *Pensées* provide another good example to remember. The great philosopher and theologian (1623–62) made notes for his works on religion and other subjects, which collected, have had a powerful influence on thought. The arrangement of the hundreds of fragmentary thoughts has always been a task that has engaged the attention of many editors for 300 years. An erudite French editor, Louis Lafuma, has decided that the text of copy 9203 in the Bibliothèque Nationale is the most reliable. Hence the decision of the editor of *Everyman* to have a new English translation of the *Pensées* done from Lafuma's second edition which was published in Paris, 1953; the translation will be found in EML, by John Warrington, with an introduction by Louis Lafuma, Dent, 1960, this being generally accepted as the closest we shall get to a definitive edition. Here the work of Louis Lafuma would be regarded as that of a rédacteur and his edition a redaction.

Reference Book is one that is not read through, but is referred to from time to time. It may seem strange that I have thought it necessary to include such an obvious term in a glossary, but it has been given a place here because I have heard it misused or not properly understood by experienced booksellers who appear to term any non-fiction book not for popular reading a 'reference book', probably echoing some old-fashioned trade term of the Victorian generation of booksellers. Of course, every book may be used by someone, at some time, as a reference book, just to check a point; equally, it will be agreed that even a dictionary is read right through, page by page, by those with the interest and leisure to do so. But so far as I know, only the fictional 'Hampdenshire Wonder', created by J. D. Beresford, has ever read right through the complete *Encyclopaedia Britannica*, a feat he accomplished in a few days of steady application, finding the work in its entirety 'rather elementary'. So, we have quick reference books and desk books, of which *Whitaker's Almanack* and language dictionaries are obvious examples; and the other class of reference books, many of which are, or should be, household books, and compilations for prolonged systematic study by students mastering a complicated subject.

Series is a publishers' term, the characteristics being uniformity of format, and sometimes of price; similarity of treatment in that individual authors are required to conform to a pattern imposed on the series by the general editor. Examples have been cited in many of the sections above, and may extend in range from an encyclopaedic subject coverage as in the *Teach Yourself* series to smaller series of monographs, such as the biographical *Great Lives*, published by Duckworths. *World's Classics, Collins, Nelson Classics*, and *Everyman* (EML) are in a class of their own, specializing in the classics and standard books in creative literature, belles lettres, history, philosophy, fiction, and children's books.

Signature belongs to the world of printing and bookbinding, for it is the printer's letter of the alphabet (sometimes a numeral is used) placed at the bottom of the first page of each section. It facilitates the making up of the complete book in the binding office; it used to be checked for correct sequence throughout the book before a copy was accepted by a librarian as a perfect book. In other words it helps one to collate the book (see *Collation* above). Still of great importance in antiquarian bookshops, where rare or scarce books are checked for imperfections before purchase and sale.

Standard Edition is related to *Definitive Edition*, which see above. A publisher and editor offer an edition of a classic as a standard one, but not necessarily a definitive one. Nevertheless, the distinction is often slight, because these editions are scholarly, provide introductions, editorial notes, etc., but are not necessarily critical editions. Hence the chief distinction. Examples: the *Oxford Standard Authors* series (OSA), in which many of the texts are based on or even the same as, those in the definitive series (OET). See publisher's descriptive note at headings in the *Oxford General Catalogue*. Standard biographies are particularly subject to 'time's fell hand'; classic biographies never. No subsequent biography can displace the classic stature of

Southey's *Nelson* for example, though as a biography it has been superseded by Carola Oman's standard work; but Henry Craik's *Swift* (1882; 1894), for long the standard biography, is superseded by Irvin Ehrenpreis's life, two volumes, 1962–1967.

Textbook indicates a treatment of a subject in a systematic style, suitable for prolonged study, section by section, in class or privately. It is differentiated from an *Introduction*, or a *Handbook* (*Manual*) by the fact that the author does not set out to offer original thought resulting from individual research, but instead takes his readers through a course of study based on a published syllabus in preparation for an examination, or for more difficult handbooks and monographs. Textbooks are seldom read through for enjoyment.

Textus receptus is a text which is generally accepted, although there may be unsolved cruces. Example: some passages in Chaucer's works.

Variorum Edition should provide the text of a work – usually a classic work of poetry, but not always – with the editorial notes of various commentators. The term is, alas, misused in America, where scholars who should know better offer as a variorum edition what is in fact an edition with variant readings, that is of textual variants. Latinists have pointed out the derivation of the term, the dictionary defines it, indicating the grammatical form and derivation (genitive plural) from the full phrase used on the title pages of eighteenth-century works of scholarship '. . . *editio cum notis variorum*'; and there seems no excuse therefore when we find Peter Allt and Russell K. Alspach as joint editors of an important edition of the *Poems* of W. B. Yeats, in a quarto of 884 pages (Macmillan, 1957) describing their impressive work as 'The Variorum Edition', when in fact it is a variant edition, or *varia lectio*, giving the poet's own variations, textual changes, and alterations in the text of some of his poems during the period from their first composition to their final appearance in his definitive *Collected Poems*, Macmillan, 1933; 1950. Similarly, no less a publisher than Oxford University Press (via, it should be admitted, Pennsylvania) has a 'Variorum' edition of *The Origin of Species*, edited by Morse Peckham, 1959, when in fact, again, this is a textual variant edition. Darwin's final revised and corrected edition was the sixth of 1872; his first was published in 1859: the development and change in his theory may therefore be charted by noting his differing texts through each edition. This is what is done in Morse Peckham's edition. Other editions in standard series, by the way, either reprint the 1859 text, or the last of 1872, a point of some importance to remember when executing an order for the book without specification by the customer. It is better always to supply the final text editions. An example of a true variorum edition is the great *Variorum Edition of the Works of William Shakespeare*, edited by H. H. Furness, Philadelphia, J. B. Lippincott Co., 27 vols., 1871– in progress as the *New Variorum Shakespeare*, 1928–. Before this we had Boswell's Variorum edition, 21 vols., 1821, itself based on Malone's of 1790, and rightly advertised as containing 'the corrections and illustrations of various commentators'. In brief, the *New Variorum* presents a complete history of Shakespearean criticism from Johnson's time to ours.

The attention here given to these familiar terms indicates how necessary it is for booksellers (and publishers) to be acquainted with the terminology of bibliography, especially in this second half of a century of specialization and development unprecedented in the history of mankind, bringing with it new demands on every section of the community serving the advancement of knowledge and learning. University bookshops are initiated every year, the student population increases, the layman becomes more informed; these and other developments demand precise, informed service from everyone working in the world of books.

QUESTIONS FOR RECAPITULATION

1. What is the difference between a standard edition and a definitive edition? Cite two examples of each.

2. Write defining, descriptive notes on a parallel text, a plain text, a handbook, and an introduction.

3. Write brief notes on examples of a redaction, a recension, a colophon, an imprint, a critical edition, and a variorum edition.

4. How does a glossary differ from a dictionary? Give examples.

5. Discuss critically three back-list or general catalogues of well-known publishers that you are familiar with.

6. Name six standard publishers' series.

Part Two
Method; Technique; Assessment of New Books

Chapter 11
Subject Booklists and Methods of Bibliographic Search

Students who have pursued the subject thus far are now well equipped to proceed to the study of practical methods in the technique of the search for records of publication, the choice of books for customers in need of advice, and the extension of this service to the compilation of subject booklists; or buying lists and shopping lists, if you like these terms better than subject bibliographies. Shopping lists they must be if the cost of the service is to be justified and the bookseller to remain in profitable business. Quoting once again from the NBA Judgment, as reported in the *Bookseller*, 3rd November 1962, p. 1832, I draw attention to the paragraph headed '*Onerous and Expensive*' in which it is stated that the service to be described in this chapter 'is onerous to provide and expensive in effort, time and money. Members of the public not unnaturally show a marked propensity to vagueness and to bibliographical inaccuracy when they ask for books'. The learned Judge, thus speaking with such accuracy that he might well have been a bookseller himself, went on to say: '. . . it must be appreciated that to provide such a service the bookseller must be equipped with an elaborate apparatus of catalogues and reference books and that skill and constant attention are required to keep this up to date. Moreover, the operation of such a service demands a considerable degree of skill and technical knowledge on the part of those employed in the bookshop, as well as tact and patience.'

The skill and knowledge so properly emphasized can only be fully acquired in the field: that is, by work in a busy bookshop and a large wholesale bookseller's warehouse. But the process of learning and the full attainment to a high degree of skill may be greatly speeded up if the subject is studied theoretically as well as practically. That is the reason for the BA's educational activities and for the courses of study for which this book (part textbook, part handbook) has been prepared.

Although the problems arising from the average customer's vagueness are becoming more and more pressing owing to the increase in the book population of the world, the complexity of subjects, and the pressure of daily work, the difficulties are not new. They go back in England to the days of Elizabeth I, when booksellers were publishers, and when tradesmen who sold books at a fixed place of business were known because of this as stationers, to distinguish them from the chapmen who did business as pedlars. By way of historical diversion, I will quote from the only reprint of a rare book in the British Museum, entitled *The Parlement of Pratlers* . . . written by John Eliot, 1593. This is a series of dialogues illustrating daily life in Elizabethan London, printed in the original edition in parallel text: English – French. It is an early example of a method of learning a foreign language, still exemplified in *Harrap's Bilingual series*, mentioned in chapter ten. One of the dialogues in this diverting book is entitled the *Bookseller*. And the talk is between the tradesman with his books for sale, and two customers, or rather, what we should call 'browsers'.

'*Booke-seller*: Buy some new booke sir, there are the last newes from France. What bookes buy you? . . . Honest man what booke lack you?
'*Man*: I must buy a certaine book but I cannot hit of the name of it.
'*Booke-seller*: Is it in verse or in prose?
'*Man*: No, no, it is a historie. Have you not some pretie little book to read in the chimnie corner?'

And so on. Thus the customer we serve tomorrow, who 'cannot hit of the name of it' is forgetful in a well-established tradition recognized in London four hundred years ago.

There are a few rules to note before we spend any time at all on a search, or proceed to select a book for a vague customer. Our Elizabethan 'booke-seller' points the sure way to one:

Find out at once exactly what your customer wants. Tactfully insist on his making up his mind; lead him firmly but slyly to the specific point.

That is, if he asks, as he so often does, for a list of 'technical' books, find out the exact branch of technology he is interested in. More often than not it will become apparent that what he really wants is a book on diesel engines or automobile engineering or some other specific subject. There are certain terms (technical is one of them) commonly used by vague customers which are so general in application that they convey little or nothing to the bookseller who may be asked to recommend a suitable book. 'Engineering' is another. Almost everything now except confectionery and the care of children, or so it seems, is engineering, from making nylons to building reactors.

If you do not succeed in this endeavour, or if you are trying to help a foreign customer whom you cannot question personally, do not hesitate to give the wrong answer in order to attract the right question.

I do not mean to suggest that you send a book through the post, hoping your choice will chance to be the right one. But if your correspondent asks you to recommend, for example, a few books on the theatre, you could give him details of some standard histories of the theatre; and if your experience is the same as mine you will in due course receive a letter of thanks, with the specific request: 'But these are not the kind of books I want; what I really require are some books on production, make-up for the stage, lighting and similar matters – not too advanced.' Then you can proceed with the enquiry, you've won your point and you may have trained your customer, without his realizing it.

When recommending certain classes of books, it is necessary to obtain clear instruction about the standard or grade required. This applies especially to school books ordered for use in a foreign country, and to the scientific classes (DC 500–600).

Thus, do not recommend without thought Trevelyan's *History of England* because you have it in stock and are aware of its quality. Your customer may be served better by *A History of Britain*, by Carter and Mears, OUP.

Beware of finding what you seek. That is, be careful of assuming from the titles of books you haven't handled, and do not stock, that they deal with the subjects you are working on for a subject book-list.

For example, it would be unwise to add to a booklist dealing with biographies and critical appreciations of the novelist Henry Fielding (1707–1754) a book such as *Fielding*, by M.

Stewart, because this is a book on cricket. The example I quote
is not an imaginary or cautionary one; it happened. The only
error approaching the 'howler' category I have ever come
across in the almost impeccable Sonnenschein (see chapter
six) is the inclusion under the heading 'Joseph Conrad' of a
book entitled *Conrad In Quest of his Youth*, by Leonard Merrick,
which is a delightful, and unjustly forgotten novel, with no
bearing on Joseph Conrad at all. Many other instances will
occur to you and there is no need for me to stress the point
further, beyond giving one additional example, in which an
assistant inadvertently added to a short list of books on
dermatology, the Italian novel *La Pelle*, by 'Curzio Malaparte'
(Rome, 1949), because it was available in an English translation as *The Skin*. Research workers in science are well aware of
the dangers of finding what they seek; and bibliographers
engaged in search work have to be equally cautious.

By extension we must often insist on going a little deeper than
the title before recommending books that do not indicate scope,
limitations, applications, and allied information, often indeed,
adequately set forth in a subtitle which, alas, is not always
provided by publishers' cataloguers when preparing their
back lists. They do not realize how useful that additional
information can be; their authors do, otherwise they would
not have given their books explanatory subtitles. There are
exceptions. One has to exercise care, otherwise one will
recommend *A Teacher's Handbook of Geography for the Primary
School*, by Glyn Davies, without realizing that it is a teacher's
training course specially compiled for use in Nigeria.

Search Technique

Speed and accuracy are the two chief requirements. A fumbling
search by inexperienced assistants may not only be un-
productive, but may also lead to an inaccurate answer, or the
impatient dismissal of an enquiry that would have produced
profitable business. Stock-holding booksellers must do their
duty with integrity, and be prepared to assist customers in
their choice of books, but must themselves be aided by trained,
alert, and informed assistants. Some of the answers given in
response to enquiries must necessarily be unrewarding, in that
they will not enable the bookseller to supply the books searched

for; but let us remember that there is some value in the negative answer for, provided it is accurate, the information will prevent further waste of time. Before we can inform a customer that we cannot supply the book required because it is o.p., we have to make sure that it is so; if we shrug the enquiry away from us, merely by refusing and neglecting to track it down, the search may still go on in other quarters, perhaps even in other departments of our own firm.

To make this sort of service practicable, assistants must cultivate good memories; develop a flair for the quest; be on the look-out for methods of elimination of the unlikely sources of information; and conversely, be quick enough on the uptake to recognize the obvious and best sources. They must be as astute as a detective in recognizing the real books beneath a layer of clerical and oral errors. Most booksellers have a collection of these. Only experience and an interest in the work can set the inner mind in motion, but solved, the problem brings its own satisfaction, and does enable us to do what we are paid for and expected to do: sell more books to the people with money in their pockets which they wish to spend on buying books, if only they knew how, or the right ones to buy.

An element of luck as well as a detective's memory enters into the chase: for example, an order for *The Idea of a Great Factory*, by Abercrombie, could be expected to puzzle any bookman who had not had the good fortune to read Lascelles Abercrombie on *The Idea of Great Poetry* when that excellent little book was available in the Martin Secker edition of 1925. Here was an example of the value of the negative answer, as well as the advantage of a perceptive memory. It did not sell a book; but it did stop a time-wasting search. An assistant might well have looked for Abercrombie on factories, beginning with the current week's *Bookseller*, working back to *Books in Print* and at least two volumes of CBL. Moreover, when a few weeks later, with the joke still fresh in people's minds, a further order was received, this time translated by a typist into *The India of Great Poets*: Abercrombie, everybody concerned recognized it at once. Obviously, this is a book for which there is a small demand, but which is doomed to clerical distortion.

On the other hand the German who asked for the original English text of a play 'by a well-known modern writer'; English title unknown; 'but no doubt you will recognize it by a

8

literal translation of its German title, which is *Once More We Have Escaped*' could scarcely have expected to receive by return Thornton Wilder's *The Skin of Our Teeth* had he realized how remote were the two idioms. Here indeed 'had he hit of the name of the author' he would have helped us considerably. Truly 'thou art translated' we may echo when we recognize 'Friends in English Poetry' for *Trends in English Poetry*; 'Guntaloni: the Courtier' for the EML steady seller Castiglione: *The Boke of the Courtier*; Huxley's 'Revolution' for *Evolution*; 'Bridie' by John Knox as the reverse of what was wanted. Certainly the morning post was brighter than normal when it included an order for 'Three Copies of Gote: Sorrows of Weather', and although, as we gazed out of the window at the English summer rain lashing the panes it seemed a pity we could not supply the books so called, we were quite pleased to remember that some enterprising publisher had recently reprinted a translation of Goethe's sentimental *Sorrows of Werther*. Remembering Thackeray's amusing parody

> Werther had a love for Charlotte
> Such as words could never utter;
> Would you know how first he met her?
> She was cutting bread and butter

vaguely reminded us of Byron, so that when the same post revealed an order for 'The Cynical Works of Lord Byron' and any good book 'on the massage of Plato' as well as Byron's drama 'Pain', life indeed seemed much more sunny inside the office than out.

On the other hand *Boil Carrots* would never have been correctly guessed as *Poil de Carotte*, had we not enjoyed the poignant little story by Jules Renard (1900). After that, 'Arctic Hay' by Huxley was simple; 'Aristotle's Latest' quickly solved; and Ingenious 'On the Sublime' at once sent us to the Loeb Classical Library list. 'Bruno and Sylvie by Nurse Carol' was of course child's play; identification of 'Catholic Missiles' a trifling affair; 'Dante's Iolanthe' scarcely raised a smile, although 'St Simeon Skylines' did. One thought his fifth-century attempt at lofty isolation to get away from it all might perhaps have been worth while.

But enough. It will be apparent to customers who may hear of these examples, that the words of Mr Justice Buckley, already quoted, apt as they were, and welcome evidence of sympathy in high places for our bibliographic problems, scarcely seem adequate to booksellers serving customers from every quarter of the globe on the narrowest margin of profit in retail trade.

The Subject Approach

This is the contemporary approach, because the present is an age of specialization. Customers' requests vary from the simple, singular: 'Have you a book, or is there one you can recommend and get for me on . . .'; to the librarian's or trade customer's complicated, comprehensive: 'Can you let me have a complete list of all the standard books now available on . . .'. For the first type, the short answer, if it indeed has to be looked up, is usually found in *British Books in Print* and CBL. When this first search produces no satisfactory title, try a source of special information, judging according to the nature of the enquiry what this would be, and whether you will be justified in pursuing the matter. If you have BNB, with its subject index cumulations, you are likely to shorten your quest, because the subject approach to books is best made via a subject classification with specific index. The classification method, as explained in a previous chapter, pin-points the specific topic to which each book is a contribution, and by means of analytical entries, extends the pointer to subsidiary subjects covered sufficiently to justify this. Examples are numerous, but I must limit my citation.

If you were asked: 'Has there been a new book lately on the plays of Ben Jonson' or if such an enquiry were put in another way, as it frequently is: 'Can you tell me the price of that new book on Ben Jonson I remember reading about a few years back?' you would be helped in your search only by a classified bibliography such as BNB, or a dictionary catalogue with full subject entries such as CBI. The reason? Because the book in question had a title giving no indication of its subject. *The Broken Compass*, by Edward Partridge, Chatto and Windus, 1958, is a critical study of some importance of the major comedies of Ben Jonson, although unfortunately the publisher's catalogue does not tell you so. But reference to BNB will direct you by means of the subject entry 'Jonson, Ben: Criticism . . . 822.3' to the class entries for that dramatist, where you will find the explanatory subtitle.

A classified source of information prevents your inclusion of inappropriate titles on subject lists; yet at the same time it enables you to pick up details of the sort of books you are looking for which you might otherwise overlook. Bibliographers building up a short list of books in print on, for example Alaska, won't find many titles by looking under that heading in catalogues, as the literature of the subject is relatively small. All the more important, therefore, not to omit such an excellent book as *Moonlight at Midday*, by Sally Carrighar, Michael Joseph, 1959, later a paperback reprint, for this is a personal narrative of Alaskan travel, although again, the publisher's catalogue does not tell us so. Obviously we are expected to carry that knowledge in our heads, along with similar awareness of the subject matter of more than a quarter of a million other books in print. Our only hope of netting so good a book (and of persuading our subject list enquirer to buy it) is to make sure we have our attention drawn to it by BNB. As the booklist compiler with access to that work would proceed direct to DC 917.98 and 979.8 (the travel class number and the corresponding history number for Alaska), he would not only be able to list this book, but would also find (in the same year) Lois Crisler's *Arctic Wild*, Secker and Warburg.

A method of indicating the relationship between two studies, or the application of one subject to another, frequently helps in the compilation of booklists. In DC this relationship is shown in a kind of shorthand by a colon so that the symbol 510:620 means applied mathematics, for the first number indicates mathematics, the second engineering. When we had to find a dozen or so books on Religious Training in Youth Clubs, we found this of great value as a rapid method of netting such a book as *Prayer Time with Youth*, by Dr L. P. Barnett, Epworth Press, 1956, which is a book of thirty orders of worship for youth clubs, taking the class number in DC of 264.1:369.4. This seems rather a long symbol, but broken down it is a simple combination of the number for Prayer and Public Worship, with that for Youth Clubs. Similarly, as the class number for Bookselling is 655.56, one could classify *Bibliography in the Bookshop* either at 655.56: 010 or 010:655.56, according to one's own preference and practice.

It will be obvious that I regard BNB as indispensable to the bibliographer, and those who use it constantly will have many other examples to add to the few I have described above. One or two additional examples may however be useful to those who are unfamiliar with it. At 12.55 one morning a film company telephoned for details to enable them to order several copies of 'a serious book about drug addiction, published perhaps six months ago'. At 12.57 (with no recollection of such a book to help her) an assistant telephoned the information required, because she was able to consult a cumulation of that year's BNB under 364.157 Drug Addiction where was indexed a book entitled *Who Live In Shadow*, by J. M. Murtagh and Sara Harris, McGraw-Hill; and in this country W. H. Allen. It was beyond doubt the right book, because the enquirer did remember 'there was something about "Shadows" in the title'.

Owing to the detail with which BNB index is compiled, sometimes it will be this, and not the classification that provides the clue: the account of the sinking of the submarine *Thetis* is the subject of *The Admiralty Regrets* . . ., published by Harrap, 1958; the index has entries for both the title and the name, as well as a subject entry under 'Submarines'. In general the more elusive the title, the more one relies on BNB to help; the deeper the pitfall, the greater the value of the classification symbol. You want to find a book to recommend to a tourist visiting the Bahamas, and not without reason think you've found one. It has the title *The Bahama Islands*; but to make sure, before you do recommend it, you check it in BNB, and to your surprise find it is classified not under some class number in 900, where the topographical books you are looking for will be, but under 797.14. This warns you off quickly, for the placing of the volume by the expert BNB classifiers at Yachting, indicates at once that it is a yachtsman's handbook.

You are making a booklist of everything in print by Edward Lear: simple. You are asked to add to it, every book in print about Lear: tricky. But with the help of BNB, which brings books to the surface very quickly once you have mastered the art of dipping your search bucket in the well of information buried in its pages, you very soon come across *The Field of Nonsense*, by Elizabeth Sewell, Chatto, 1952. It is exactly the kind of book you are after, because it discusses the whole art, giving considerable attention to Lear as well as Lewis Carroll. One of your assistants is listing all the novels by L. A. G. Strong still in print, and includes *Flying Angel*; but wary from long experience, you give instructions for the BNB entry to be checked first. If the book is at 823.91 (British Fiction: Contemporary) O.K., if not, delete it from your draft. As *Flying Angel* is found to be at 387.5 (Merchant Navy) you know without further enquiry that this is a non-fiction book which the novelist did on the Missions to Seamen, giving it an appropriate title.

Once your familiarity with DC is known to distant and library customers you will occasionally receive orders such as this, which came in a cable from Lima, Peru: 'Are there books DC 629.138:639?' Decoded, this reads, 'Are there any books on the subject of the use of aircraft for whaling?' 629.138 is Use of Aircraft for Special Purposes; the colon indicates the purpose, for 639 is DC for Whaling. And there was one reference under this number, for a book with the sort of title that conceals its subject matter. Or a librarian in a hurry to open a branch library will ask: 'Please send me about 400 popular books on the following subjects, not more than 3 different titles covering one subject.' Then will follow not a list of subjects but a list of DC numbers. This helps you to select quickly books not in stock; it ensures that the library stock will be balanced and ready to meet a variety of demands.

Finally, as one is frequently asked to give details for a buying list of recent novels, translated from . . . it may be Italian, or Russian, or Lithuanian, or Finnish . . . any literature in fact, the search is speedy, can be entrusted to a beginner, and does not depend on memory. In BNB translations of foreign literature are classed under the national number; thus 833.91 means modern German fiction in translation; 843.91 French; 843: Italian; 863: Spanish; 891.92: Lithuanian; and so on for every language. A typist has merely to copy the entries from three or four annual cumulations for the required language, and the job is done.

Students are urged to revise the material in chapter seven, to make sure that they are thoroughly familiar with this useful feature, and the other, equally quick method of compiling lists of biographies and autobiographies of specified classes of people, such as doctors, scientists, economists, etc.

The Use of Specialized Sources of Information, and Reference Books, as Short Cuts

I do not suggest that all the books mentioned in the final

section of this chapter will be available in the average bookshop and its search office, but again stress the value of making full and frequent use of the public reference library, either by personal call or by telephoned enquiry. For example, it is not infrequent to receive orders for texts of plays, and books on the theatre, a subject characterized by anthologies and collections. The searcher in difficulties must here always remember to take the short cut to the answer, by making use of the most comprehensive bibliography of the subject readily available. It is known as *The Player's Library*, and as a catalogue of the largest and most comprehensive collection of plays and books on the theatre in Great Britain is virtually a bibliography of the theatre. The principal volume was published by Faber in 1950; followed by supplements, all published for the British Drama League. This source of bibliographical information extends to more than 1,500 pages, many entries supply names of publishers, all give dates, and the contents of collections and anthologies are listed. It not only gives details of thousands of plays, but also includes within its scope books on the theatre, biographies of stage personalities, books on scenery, lighting, production, and dramatic criticism, with a title index of the plays, and in the supplementary volumes a section devoted to plays in French, with a separate index. I have found in practice that it answers without fail, every question ever raised by a customer requiring books on these related subjects. Certainly if it failed me, I should consider it unlikely that further search would be justified. Similarly with that other specialized source, mentioned in an earlier chapter: the catalogue of H. K. Lewis's *Medical, Scientific and Technical Library*. Here the coverage in the two last categories cannot be as complete as the medical section, but since most of the enquiries which make it an indispensable source refer to medical science or some branch of it, I would put it next to *The Player's Library* in importance as a short cut.

Now let us turn to a quite different set of reference books, one or two of which might well be in all large bookshops. I refer to *Who's Who*, and its complementary series of *Who Was Who*; to Chambers's *Biographical Dictionary* and similar biographical reference books. *Who's Who* and its chronological predecessors provide concise biographies of authors of books as well as other important people, and as authors are asked by the editors to provide dated lists of their publications, here we have an authoritative and handy short cut when searching for a certain type of information. The six volumes of *Who Was Who* take the record back to 1897, bringing it to 1970 in the last one published. But it is the current *Who's Who* which is usually the issue likely to be of most use, and to which we may turn at once if we receive an order or any enquiry for a book by a well-known author, and yet with a title quite unfamiliar to us. Such books will be listed in *Who's Who* entries with dates of publication, enabling us to check immediately with the CBL, or other annual list, for publisher. From this annual list we turn at once to the publisher's current stock list. Even if we have to offer our customer only a negative answer we do so with some confidence and finality. Often the *Who's Who* entry will quote the English titles of foreign works. This helped once to supply a book by Pierre Mendès-France (*Liberté; liberté; chérie*) Englished in 1956 as *The Pursuit of Freedom*.

Soon after the death of the composer Vaughan Williams, a BBC programme referred to poems by his wife; one of these was read, and it attracted a number of enquiries for a book with 'The Poems of Mrs. Vaughan Williams'. No such book could then be traced. But before giving the negative answer we looked up the entry in the current *Who's Who*, from which we learnt the maiden name of the composer's wife, Ursula Wood, and thus succeeded in tracing several books by her. Later a volume was published by Hutchinson enabling the entries in BNB to be cross-referenced between the two names.

I mentioned Chambers's *Biographical Dictionary* above because an admirable feature of this standard work is the citation at the end of each entry, of biographical monographs on the individual subjects. In the latest, revised edition of 1968, this material has been brought up to date. Thus if you are asked for publisher and price of a standard biography of Thomas Gainsborough, to quote a chance example, you will find that a quick reference to Chambers's will tell you that a life and study of the painter was published in 1958 by Waterhouse, and that Sir Joshua Reynolds's 14th Discourse is worth consulting. A swift glance at CBL for 1958 informs you that the book was published by Hulton Press.

Do not overlook annual surveys of literature given in *Whitaker's Almanack* and the *Annual Register*: they help in the

rapid compilation of lists of key books for specific years, sometimes asked for by foreign customers wishing to check holdings
of English books for gaps; these reference books are also useful
for details of literary prizewinners from the most famous of all,
the Nobel prizes for literature, to recently initiated prizes.

For extra-mural sources of specialized information booksellers
should add to their reference books the latest edition of *Scientific
and Learned Societies of Great Britain*: a handbook compiled from
official sources, Allen and Unwin. Many of these societies have
offices in London, nearly all have libraries, and provided one
does not make unreasonable requests, information officers are
usually obliging enough to help. They are often able to do so at
once: for I had a difficult enquiry to answer quickly from an
important customer, relating to a new book on some obscure
scientific subject which we could not trace. We were assured
that the book was available in English and that it was a most
important monograph. The enquiry was worth pursuing, so we
obtained particulars of the society most likely to have knowledge of the work, telephoned, and were given the information
immediately: 'Yes, we have the book here; it has been translated
into English; but you will have to order it from Moscow, and
wait about a month to get it.' Well might we have searched in
vain and have been unjustly depreciated by our customer, had
we not been able to call upon this specialized source of information. Such service is two-way, and it is always a pleasure to be
able to give information in response to requests from those who
have so courteously helped us.

Only long experience in this type of work can teach one the
technique of the elimination of the unlikely and concentration
on the most likely source, but from the few examples I have
cited I hope to have given hints and indicated sufficiently the
possibilities. Sometimes one has to guess what a foreign customer means, but do not be superior if the English used by,
say, an oriental trade customer, is unlike your own idiom;
after all, he is writing better in English than you can in say,
Japanese, when you try to reply in his language, if you make the
attempt, which is doubtful. So if you receive a request for a list
of a dozen good English books on 'Making the best use of
existing facilities' make the effort to guess what is wanted, and
send the wrong answer if you cannot, in order, as I have
recommended above, to attract the right question. In this case

details of some popular books on self-help, personal psychology, and similar topics proved to be what was wanted. We were a little more doubtful about sending the same list to the customer from Nigeria who wanted books on 'Seizing Time by the Forelock', but it turned out satisfactorily. On the other hand we hesitated to answer a request from the Middle East for British books on 'Double Dealing', although the Suez Affair was still fresh in one's mind. Here we hedged by suggesting books on card games. Wide of the mark, the guess eventually produced a specific request for some British books on buying wholesale and selling retail.

Every bookseller perhaps has his own list of such light-hearted attempts to satisfy a world of customers. Certainly one feels that the information office of such an experienced society as the National Book League may one day fill an amusing page or two in a trade magazine with similar and better examples.

Every bookseller subscribes to and supports the National Book League: its information office is one important source of bibliographical information: extra-mural, but still, closer to our shops even than the local public library. One hopes that the 1970's will bring even more young assistants to the doors of number Seven Albemarle Street, using its resources, helping its imaginative ventures in the cause of book publicity, and supporting it financially by personal membership.

Always complicated and costly, the business of book service and search grows more so every few years. In the last decade alone, we have had from Europe, USA and in this country, great catalogues of expensive but extremely valuable reprints of scarce, antiquarian books. New processes of printing and reproduction have made this possible, but who knows now, what really is in print and what is out of print at any given week of the year?

We must insist on the institutional customer with time, money, staff and bibliographical apparatus helping the bookseller to the full with his specialized orders. We must never overlook the value of these extra-mural sources of information even to the aristocrats of the book trade.

QUESTIONS FOR RECAPITULATION

1. What is meant by the term 'extra-mural sources of information' when used in the book trade? Give some examples.

2. What type of literary information, sometimes useful to a bookseller, can be obtained from *Whitaker's Almanack,* the *Annual Register, Who's Who,* Chambers's *Biographical Dictionary*?

3. Explain how a knowledge of Dewey Decimal Classification is useful to booksellers.

Chapter 12
Basic Stock and the Assessment of New Books

This concluding chapter of the second part of the course will indicate the nature of those questions calling for practical experience in a bookshop, especially in the selection of books for a basic stock, subscribing new books offered day by day by publishers' representatives, and allied topics concerned with display and layout. Some of these topics are allocated to other sections of the diploma examination; the remainder will serve as an introduction to the concluding section of this textbook, which deals with a selection of standard books in each of the main classes of the Dewey classification scheme.

I would advise students to be so familiar with the layout of a first-class bookshop as to be able to draw a plan from memory, and to write a concise description in a few hundred words of its important features. This shop may be the one worked in; it may not be; but those students who select such a question must be equipped to answer it from first-hand knowledge. Go into a large, well-stocked bookshop with notebook in hand: take note of the type of shelving; the display stands; the arrangement or group classification; and the placing of cash desk; paperbacks; current fiction; do-it-yourself and domestic subjects; the best-selling books of the month; and the difficult items such as maps; Bibles; guide books; reference books; art books; and dictionaries. Much of this may appear to be commonsense, but one does come across ill-arranged shops. If your ideal arrangement is qualified by local or special circumstances, say so. This is certain to attract additional marks, as it will be taken as a sign of individuality, freedom from routine application of general rules, and as a display of good sense based on experience.

Conventional classes as used in the trade for many generations, similar to those adopted in 'classified' trade bibliographies, are suitable for the majority of shops with a general trade. That is, the customer expects to find current travel literature and guide books near each other, with maps near by. He likes to go straight to the gardening section, and if the do-it-yourself handyman type of book is adjacent may extend his interest to this related topic. If the stock in biographies is sufficient to justify a separate grouping, the bookseller will have to choose between haphazard arrangements; or an alphabetical sequence by author; or by the subject of the biographies. I favour the last. Many customers will remember that there is a new book on Layard, or Sir Richard Burton, or D. H. Lawrence, without recalling the author. Usually the subject is paramount, but series are certainly best kept together, overriding subject matter.

In brief, I would say that good display and bookshop classification is largely a mixture of commonsense, copycat, and convention. But first-class booksellers do not hesitate to break all the rules on occasion. Basic stock requires different treatment from the books of the month. Topical interest will often focus attention on an item from basic stock, justifying a special 'out-of-group' display. Answers should draw attention to these points, concentrating on the set pattern, but emphasizing the necessity for unconventional treatment according to the book, the type of trade, and the topics of the day.

To understand this question of display from the customer's point of view, and the allied question of service, read the objective report and documented criticism in *Books and Reading* by Dr Peter H. Mann and J. L. Burgoyne (André Deutsch, 1969), especially chapter four on *A Survey of Bookshops*. This book may possibly annoy you. If it does, it has surely fulfilled its function.

Basic stock for a large city shop will scarcely be suitable for a quiet suburban trade. Therefore it is necessary to answer questions on this subject with careful attention to the type of shop you have in mind, qualifying your suggestions in order to ensure that the examiner will see that you have a commonsense approach to this all-important topic. Day-by-day acquaintance with the stock of a good bookshop and a good memory for the type of books described in the final section of this course should equip all students with the essential knowledge.

You may work in a city bookshop where you would be quite right to insist that the *Shorter Oxford Dictionary* must be regarded as basic; but you would scarcely wish to keep it on your shelves in a London suburban shop. A good plan is to sketch out the précis of an answer under headings: Basic Series, Popular

Non-Fiction, Standard Reference Books, Perennial Favourites in Fiction, the same type in Children's Books, when not dealt with under series; standard technical books suited perhaps to a locality, seasonal books for students taking courses of instruction, such as examinations preparation, and so on. When you have made such a list you can proceed to answer your question by giving an indication under each heading of the sort of books you have in mind.

Thus, having stated clearly the type of bookshop you are proposing in theory to stock, under basic series you would briefly mention *Teach Yourself*, and the four great classics series: EML, *Worlds Classics*, Collins, Nelson, indicating by selection of a few titles that you are fully aware of the popular and special books you would expect to find in all good shops. Mention a few of Dent's *Children's Illustrated Classics*; note the standard editions of Lewis Carroll; list a few popular authors of the best books for young readers; and so on, through your headings. Such a question takes time; it will, however, earn good marks if tackled thoroughly. Do not attempt it if you feel pressed for time or too ill-equipped. You have a fair choice.

Assessment of New Books

Questions on this all-important section of the daily life of a bookseller often take the form of asking for your opinion about new art books, new dictionaries, new historical works, offered for subscription. You may be asked to list in order of importance the points you would check and inspect before giving your stock order. Largely a matter of commonsense, these decisions are usually made by buyers with long experience, but you may prepare yourself for this responsibility, as well as for the examination, by testing your acumen and judgment for your own shop. Every week, select a dozen new books in various classes; list them and put your personal decision against each item, with, sometimes, a note on the factors that have influenced you in arriving at the subscription total. Then seek the critical help of your buyer; show him your list and ask for comments. You may be sure he will often differ from you and equally surely it will sometimes be he that is wrong, not you, but never remind him of this. You will be wise to remember that 'he who never overbuys must often underbuy' because the element of chance

enters through the door of judgment just when you are slam-
ming it to with an air of finality. When a buyer talks about
'a hunch', or 'flair' he is really drawing your attention to
chance. When you become a buyer you will doubtless do the
same, referring from time to time to the notable occasions when
your 'hunch' or 'flair' enabled you to anticipate public demand
for a book which to many others seemed a very ordinary affair.
In sum, looking back on a year's buying, you will have to have
been approximately right most of the time. A few chancey
successes will not offset a score of bad buys; your profit on
twenty sold copies of a £2.10 book will have to be set against
your loss if five copies remain unsold, moreover the space the
dusty five will take up on your shelves will be pushing out
more topical books.

Many booksellers reserve their special exercise of judgment
for unusual books by new authors, lavishly illustrated quartos
produced to attract a fairly easily estimated type of buyer,
striking bargains, and publications demanding salesmanship
rather than passive stock holding. The remainder of the books
offered for subscription they will buy against the record of the
authors' previous sales, this record being kept on order cards
made out for every book added to stock thus providing a complete history of buying and selling, re-ordering and final
decisions. Not a bad rule of thumb, provided the buyer will
bravely thrust it aside on occasion. He will, of course, often be
requested to do so by persuasive publishers' representatives;
but in the end, the decision must be his and he must feel con-
fident of it. Here shrewdness and a natural ability must play a
very large part, as well as long training. On such decisions
depends the future of the shop or business he is feeding with
new books. Buy it the wrong food and the patient will die.
Prudence is necessary; boldness must be often rewarded; mis-
takes admitted, even if only to oneself; and in any event, the
decisions must be supported by everybody working in the same
establishment.

It is here that the type of active bookselling we sometimes
read and hear about in the trade papers makes itself felt. The
laodicean browser may perhaps be cleverly persuaded to leave
the shop with two books (both paid for), when he entered to
buy only one. By means of a routine postcard notification the
occasional visitor may be made aware of the existence of the

very book he has been looking for. The subscriber to specialist or professional journals may have his interest aroused in a new book of substance on his vocation. This sort of salesmanship makes a shop hum with life and interest. It succeeds in selling the right book at the right time to the right customer.

Discerning buyers help to improve the standard of publishing. New firms are founded; books that should have indexes are published without that necessary aid to quick reference. Buyers who examine advance or proof copies have here an opportunity to improve a book and to make it more likely to be a success. I once saw a substantial book on paediatrics, written by a specialist, and published by a fairly well-known firm. There was no index, although the writer had prepared his handbook for busy practitioners and clinical staff. Undated books are now rare, but only because of the protests of book-sellers and librarians, who in the past have refused to buy them. Before long every book entered in a publisher's catalogue will bear the bibliographical details to enable booksellers to select, reject, and recommend certain books with confidence. Of what use is a book on life in modern Spain if we do not know the date? How is one to recommend by selection, a good book presenting a current survey of problems in China if the date is not readily available? A publisher's back list which includes a book on moon and space travel without details of date and contents must be faulted as incomplete and unsatisfactory. These are some of the points to watch; and for students to remember when dealing with that section of the examination paper.

Two classes of creative literature present the greatest dif-ficulties to buyers, and students may usefully mention them in order to display their awareness of the problem of selling first novels and modern poetry in contemporary Britain. Here more than in any other class of books caution is necessary, though pleasurable success may reward bold judgment based on individual interest and cultivated taste. Somebody had to launch *The Waste Land* in 1923. Some booksellers did buy a few copies of that four shillings and sixpenny booklet of thirty-five pages, because as a youth I remember buying one. James Joyce's *Pomes Penyeach* was a pretty little book too. So don't sweep away poetry by new writers as if it is so much dust waiting to settle on your shelves; it may be; but some of it will be gold dust. Make your choice here as balanced as it is in the buying of other books by new writers. Then do your utmost to sell what you have bought to the people you feel can be made as interested and impressed as you are by new talent. Above all, let us remember that authors make it possible for booksellers to earn their living in one of the pleasantest of all trades and if we want new books we must have new authors; let us give full credit to publishers and to their readers, who have already told us by the mere fact of publication what they think of their new writers. Your encouragement, be it ever so slight, may be multiplied by the total number of tradesmen with a similar outlook on books and authors. Your choice may influence the library buyer and through him, your local private book collectors; and through them, a whole generation of writing and thought. Such a sequence is part of your justification for your high status in a civilized community. Such a sequence the highest reward of the greatest of twentieth-century booksellers, the late John Wilson, who from his tiny office at Bumpus's helped the known and the unknown, published privately poetry now prized as the most beautiful nature poetry of our time, found time to guide the reading of the socially distinguished, served kings and queens with wisdom and wit, and by his bookmanship attracted the greatest authors of his time to buy other authors' books in his shop as well as to ask his advice about their own.

I once knew a bookseller whose enthusiasm for certain types of contemporary creative literature was so great that he found time to type unknown authors' work for them during the many hours when business was slack. One of those authors is very famous now; but when he was making a meagre living on a pound or two a week, that bookseller's help in typing manuscripts was a wonderful gesture and an encouragement of boundless worth. If your temperament is that way inclined, do the same: encourage, help, buy. Make others buy.

QUESTIONS FOR RECAPITULATION

1. Describe the arrangement and method of stock display in an ideal, one-floor bookshop serving the general public in an industrial town.

2. Publishers' representatives submit an advance copy of a new

9

street atlas of London; the first volume of a new history of Europe; a quarto of plates in colour reproduced from paintings in the National Gallery, London; a new edition of Shakespeare's *Hamlet*. Write concise, practical notes indicating your method of assessment, standards and tests, and general practice when deciding in each specific case on the question of to stock, or not to stock; to recommend or not to recommend to likely customers.

Part Three
Notes on a Knowledge of Stock and Publishers' Back Lists

Chapter 13
Dewey Classes: 0 to 200: Standard Stock

When the first edition of *Bibliography in the Bookshop* was published students were advised that this final section of four chapters was 'beyond the requirements of the Booksellers' Association diploma'. By 1970 the statement had become inaccurate, yet within the compass of an introductory course such as this, these last chapters must still be termed 'Notes'. The field of knowledge is vast; some of it can only be traversed after decades of work in large bookshops and libraries, but the minimum should be within the range of a beginner student after working through all relevant sections of the current syllabus.

Candidates for the diploma are expected to have a working knowledge of basic stock and of standard books in all classes of the Dewey main ten. How personal, how deep, how intensive that knowledge goes depends on the personal experience and interests of the individual student. But the minimum must be ability to cite correct titles and authors, publishers, approximate or actual prices, and to annotate specific choices briefly, so as to make clear their range, grades, and the types of readers most likely to find them adequate for their needs.

Beyond this outline knowledge, is the specialized, deeper acquaintance with a small group of subjects reflecting the personal interests and the daily work of booksellers. One would recommend emphatically the acquirement of specialized bibliographical knowledge to every bookshop assistant. The advantages to the business and to the customers are obvious but personal rewards may also be considerable, and the pride of the experienced bookman is worth striving for. It is the bookseller's equivalent of the craftsman's pride in the mastery of his medium and the creative impulse of the artist. Moreover, such slowly acquired knowledge has great social value in civilized societies.

Hence, in surveying the world of books for these four chapters, I shall merely be commenting on landmarks in the literary landscape, discussing them in the order established by DC. In one group of subjects, Music (class 780–789) I shall indicate a wider choice, because this will enable me to exemplify the application of the terminology explained in chapter ten.

We start with Dewey's Generalia class, because here we group books and sets of books dealing not with one or two subjects but with large, comprehensive subjects, embracing characteristically all known knowledge.

031: General Encyclopaedias: 032

Etymologically the familiar term is derived from the Greek. It signified a course of general education, and its current extended meaning, dating bibliographically from the eighteenth century, is logical and convenient. The characteristic arrangement of an encyclopaedia of general knowledge is A–Z, but examples will be cited of variants.

We may be proud of the fact that the most famous encyclopaedia in the world is still entitled *Encyclopaedia Britannica*. We may be glad that the Americanization of this great work, financially, editorially, and commercially, has extended its service to mankind throughout the English-speaking world. Defects and standards have been widely discussed: those who have the 11th edition (1911) still wisely refuse to part with it, in spite of the inadequacy of all of the articles on scientific and technical developments of the twentieth century; but for those who can afford *Encyclopaedia Britannica*, this handsome, well produced set of 24 quarto volumes (offering more than 37 million words, and about 23,000 pictures) takes first place in the library at DC 031.

The methodical revision, details of index volume, and other interesting information, together with the prices of the standard sets, will be found in the Retail Catalogue issued by the company at the beginning of each year, together with details of a tribute to the initiator of the great enterprise in the shape of a replica of the first edition of 1768–1771.

Doubtless most of the sets sold annually are by direct sale distribution, but of late years, by offering a satisfactory commission, the company has encouraged retail booksellers to attract new customers.

Next to this work in fame and importance comes *Chambers's*

Encyclopaedia (*Chambers's* for short). Not so costly, revised in 1967 and with many admirable features, this 14-volume work, in quarto, with a final volume of index and maps, is specially attractive to schools, customers whose accommodation for shelves is too small to take the larger set conveniently; branch libraries, and business houses.

The third notable work is also perhaps the most popular of all: the excellent smaller *Everyman Encyclopaedia*, fully revised in 1967 in 12 medium octavo, illustrated volumes. *Everyman* has no index volume. Why is this and why have the other two great encyclopaedias (all arranged A–Z) been provided with this feature? Students will discover this for themselves by examination and use. Here the local reference library is the easiest school to attend. Nothing is better than the first-hand knowledge of great reference books which can so easily be acquired by examination and use in the quietude of a library. This essential knowledge, when tucked away permanently in the student's mind, is for ever after at the disposal of the man with the money in his pocket to spend on home, school and business reference books, but who wisely asks for advice and reliable information before writing out his cheque.

Ignoring works of solely American origin in order to limit this discussion, but not to suggest that students should follow such an exclusion (the library is there for those who should insist on pursuing the topic), let us turn attention to a few handy encyclopaedias in one volume. Of these, the two most widely used are Hutchinson's *New Twentieth Century* and Collins's *New Age*. Each has useful features. Both are surely part of essential basic stock (when in print) and either will serve to start off a home reference library. Low price items both (Hutchinson's last edition, of 1968, is £2·50 for 1,118 pages, illustrated), they attract a popular market embracing those who have the larger works, but who need a handy desk book as well, and the beginner who wisely starts to build up a home reference library of essential books by adding an encyclopaedia, however small, to his collection.

In the one-volume category, we need not restrict ourselves to strictly British publications, for there is a unique work, rightly respected, in the *Columbia Encyclopaedia*, compiled on a vaster scale than anything we have in Britain in its class. The *Columbia* will be found in the larger reference libraries, and may be recommended with confidence as a suitable work for board rooms, chairmen's office libraries, and company secretaries. This large quarto of 7,500,000 words and 75,000 articles, is now somewhat costly (about 50 dollars for the 3rd edition). One of its many useful features is the bibliography following the most important articles, suggesting further reading and a whole library of additional sources of information, extending in effect to a bibliography of 35,000 standard books. Another is the carefully compiled series of about 80,000 cross-references, and over 60 pages of maps and drawings.

Books of general and household knowledge will be part of the stock-in-trade of all shops: *Enquire Within Upon Everything* has been with us for over a hundred years, *Pears Cyclopaedia*, Martin's *Book of General Knowledge*, the *Teach Yourself Concise Encyclopaedia* and a few others, are cheap, popular, and always helpful, occasionally supplying information lacking in larger works.

Finally, there are the junior encyclopaedias, which also include books of general knowledge, more or less systematically presented. This is a special group, worthy of full, critical attention by a small committee of booksellers and librarians. Such a project could well form the basis of a salutary article in a magazine such as *Which*. At the top comes the *Oxford Junior Encyclopaedia*, which is an extensive set of 12 volumes of general knowledge, plus an index volume. Here we have knowledge divided into 12 large classes; one class, one volume. Thus, the A–Z characteristic arrangement of an encyclopaedia having been discarded the index is, if not essential, certainly useful in schools and libraries. One advantage of this set is that single volumes may be bought separately, to the individual choice of the young reader, who may wish to include in his survey of knowledge only technical and scientific groups of subjects.

For examination purposes one would regard as a minimum acquaintance with this encyclopaedia and with such popular general books as the Ward Lock series, the *Junior Pears*, *Pears Handy Reference Book*, Macdonald's *Junior Reference Library*, and the ever-popular Black's *Children's Encyclopaedia*. Their individual features should be known by personal examination, together with their prices and arrangement.

Turning now to DC classes 100 and 200, we should first note

certain standard reference books, even though few bookshops would stock them; some well-known series and then the perennial classics.

Consider then such a one-volume quarto as the illustrated *Concise Encyclopaedia of Western Philosophy and Philosophers*, edited by James O. Urmson. This popular, yet learned work was reprinted in 1968 by Hutchinson, and it provides a remarkable summary of the lives and systems of the Western world's philosophers, with entries on the terminology of main topics connected with the subject. Contributors include notable contemporary British philosophers.

There is a vast reference literature on religion and students working in the specialist bookshops will have more than the minimum knowledge required, but what of the general bookshop assistant? What must he regard as the minimum? My own arbitrary selection would include a library knowledge of or acquaintance with the famous *Encyclopaedia of Religion and Ethics*, 13 volumes, which, as it was originally compiled by Dr J. Hastings with a team of distinguished scholars (1909–1926), is usually referred to as 'Hastings Encyclopaedia of Religion'. On examination, it will be found that the coverage is much more than religion and ethics, embracing as well, anthropology, folk lore, and even economics and biology when relevant to the main topics. Never having been superseded it has always been kept in print by T. and T. Clark, who are also the publishers of Hastings' *Dictionary of Christ and the Gospels* in two volumes and his illustrated *Dictionary of the Bible* (in revised editions over 1,000 pp. quarto).

We should not leave even this briefest of comments on the subject without a glance at the popular works such as J. D. Davis's *Westminster Dictionary of the Bible* (Collins), a *Concise Dictionary of the Bible*, issued in 1966 in two paperbacks by Lutterworth Press, a *Student's Bible Dictionary* by F. L. Lay (Hodder) and *Oxford Helps to the Study of the Bible* (OUP), which for less than a pound provides with 104 plates, and 14 maps, summaries of the several books of the Bible, with a dictionary of proper names, a biblical index, and a concordance. It is a perennial favourite with students at theological colleges.

Of the many series on religion and philosophy one may select three: the *Muirhead Library of Philosophy*, edited by Professor H. D. Lewis, for Allen and Unwin, whose catalogue should be consulted for this and many other books classified in DC 100–299. So extensive is this publisher's back list on philosophy and religion that the index runs to nine columns. In passing, one would also refer to the catalogues of Routledge, as well as the university presses, for some superficial idea of the contribution of the great publishing houses to learned and popular surveys in these classes.

From the catalogue of CUP may be gleaned information about the world-famous *Library of Living Philosophers*, a substantial series of monographs from America, at present in ten volumes, one volume one philosopher, each presenting a critical introduction, followed by the quintessence of the thought of the great thinkers of the century, Eastern and Western, together with personal statements.

The death of Bertrand Russell renders the Russell volume in this series of even greater interest because of the personal statement written for posterity about a quarter of a century ago. Here again we should remember Allen and Unwin for as the publisher of all of Russell's books the back list presents at a glance the range of the philosopher's knowledge, mind and teaching.

Our third series choice is the well-established *Wisdom of the East* to be found in John Murray's back list. These pocket introductions have no equal in their class.

Glancing at the *Oxford General Catalogue*, the student will find at the head of class 270–289 (The Christian Church History) a standard work edited by F. L. Cross: *The Oxford Dictionary of the Christian Church* (1957, 1, 512 pp.); and next to it a complementary Oxford Paperback, *Documents of the Christian Church*, selected and edited by Henry Bettenson. As a source book, it should be remembered by students of European history, and even general readers find it deeply interesting to dip into or for reference.

To end this briefest of recommended minimum knowledge, remember also *Everyman's Reference Library*, which includes a *Dictionary of Non-Classical Mythology* by Egerton Sykes.

From this group of subtopics we should now give some detailed attention to

220: The Holy Scriptures: 229

observing that the term 'bible' is not used in the text of our holy scriptures. We have now extended the word so widely that a standard selection of the scriptures of the great religions, edited by R. O. Ballou, is entitled *The Bible of the World* (Routledge, 1956, 1, 415 pp.); and if we couple this mentally with Hutchinson's *Concise Encylopaedia of Living Faiths* (1959, 432 pp., illustrated quarto) we have two good books on comparative religions to recommend.

It is suggested that the word 'bible' should be looked up in Webster's *Seventh New Collegiate Dictionary*, where the etymology is clearly set out (diminutive of Greek *byblos* – papyrus book, from Byblos, an ancient Phoenician city from which this papyrus writing material was exported – being *biblion*), and where the books of the OT and NT are set out in columns, under the Douai version, the Authorized Version; followed by the Jewish scriptures, and the Protestant Apocrypha.

Here almost, is skeleton history of a most bewildering subject. Almost, but not quite enough for the knowledgeable bookseller, who will at least need to know that up to 1961 there were six important English versions. The *Douai* (1582–1610) is, of course, the Roman Catholic Bible, so-called after the city of Douai, sometimes referred to as the *Douay-Rheims*. How does it differ from the Protestant version? First, from Webster's presentation, we notice a difference in the order of the books, and here and there, in the titles. Then, in the *Douai version*, some books (known as the *Apocrypha*) are included, some in the OT, others in the NT. In other words, these books are here accepted as canonical.

These hidden writings, 'apocrypha', were in fact never written in Hebrew, nor were they ever accepted by Jews. At the time of the Reformation they were rejected as false writings and excluded by Protestants. However, those who translated at Douai, did so from a Latin manuscript. (See the *Vulgate*, below.) As the earliest Bible manuscripts from the OT are in Hebrew, and for the NT in Greek, these writings are not to be found in all Protestant Bibles, and are often printed and published separately. Refer to the *Oxford Bible Catalogue*, or the *General Catalogue* (pp. 38–47) for the various editions, with, or without, or separately.

After the Roman world conquest, the Bible was translated into Latin (in order to help in the conversion of the Romans to the Christian faith) and it is this version, known as the *Vulgate* (from *vulgatus* – made public), which was translated, with revisions, at Douai, to become the authorized text of the Roman Catholic Bible.

Next we have the most celebrated of all English Bibles, the so-called *Authorized Version* (AV), or King James's Bible, although King James never authorized it. What he did do was to authorize a conference at Hampton Court in 1604. Here forty-seven revisers (high and low church) set to work on Archbishop Parker's 'Bishops' Bible', and thus was born in 1611 the Authorized Version in its stately, vigorous Jacobean prose, shorn of unnecessary Latinisms, and a landmark in English literature for all time.

In 1885 we had the *Revised Version* of this AV. It was the work of British and American advisory scholars in committee, convened in 1871. They were able to produce the NT in 1881 and the complete Bible four years later.

Nelson's published in 1901 an *American Revised Version*, because since 1885 there had been discovered three of the oldest bible manuscripts. It was recognized, too, that the splendid archaic language of the AV was misleading. Hence the need for revision. Students might note that revision does not imply the use of modern prose style and vocabulary. Neither the RV nor the ARV are in modern English: they are just more accurate. In the AV we come across the well-known 'a tale that is told' but this does not mean what at first we may think it does. In Jacobean usage 'tale' is related to number – today bank cashiers are still known as 'tellers' and the earlier usage still survives in the idiom: 'all told, we scored over fifty'. Thus, 'we bring our years to an end, as it were a tale that is told' reveals its true meaning only when we remember the history of the word.

Similarly, 'untold gold' takes its correct meaning in our mind only if we think of it as 'uncounted gold' . . . and so on.

It was such expressions as these that the revisers of 1901 considered in need of rephrasing. Again, new discoveries of this century affected scholars' knowledge of the New Testament, and so in 1946, we had from Nelson, a *Revised Standard Version* of the NT only. The two testaments, the OT of 1901 and the NT of the 1946 revision, became known together as the *New Revised Standard Version*, and it was this text that was put into the best-selling *Fontana* paperback of 1963. Many bookshop assistants mistook it for a new version in current English.

Of all versions in the English of today, the *New English Bible*
is of course by far the most popular. The NT was published in
March 1961; by the end of that year nearly 4,000,000 copies
had been sold throughout the world.

One may be forgiven for thinking that this colossal sale, as
evidence of world-wide interest in this greatest book of the
Western civilized world, would now and again have resulted in
some noticeable difference in the behaviour of rulers, peoples
and politicians. But one looks in vain for a sign that the teach-
ings of the New Testament expressed in plain, contemporary
English, have had the slightest effect. But progress in these
matters must necessarily be very slow.

The *New English Bible* was completed by the publication in
1970 of the Old Testament and in March of that year the one-
volume publication of the complete translation, including the
Apocrypha, was acclaimed as a triumph of collective scholarship and collaboration of the two university presses (CUP and
OUP).

Geoffrey Hunt has written a record of the principal facts
behind this extraordinary effort, and of the progress of the work
of the translators over a period of about twenty years, with its
recurring problems of vocabulary, editing and design. *About the
New English Bible* was published by the two presses in 1970.
It is of permanent value.

Other modern English translations are familiar to all booksellers. The *Moffat* version, J. B. Phillips's very popular translations of the *Gospels in Modern English*, the new best-selling
Jerusalem Bible of 1966 and an unusual addition to bible translation bibliography in the first version from the Greek text of
the NT ever to be made by a Jewish scholar. This was published
as *The Authentic New Testament* (1955). Then there is the Jewish
Bible, known to Jews as *Holy Scriptures*, rather than the Bible.
It differs from the AV and the RV. It followed the latter in 1917,
and is a translation of the Hebrew text of the Old Testament.

Reference books on this subject would fill a large library.
Hastings' *Dictionary* has already been mentioned. Every year
brings additions, such as *Who's Who in the Bible*, published in
Teach Yourself series in 1970, providing in handy format an
A–Z list of every person mentioned in the two testaments, and
in the Apocrypha; and from Oliphants comes a *Dictionary of
Bible Place Names*.

The standard popular and scholarly historical account was first published by Sir Frederic Kenyon in 1895 (*Our Bible and the Ancient Manuscripts*). Eyre and Spottiswoode published a completely revised edition in 1958. A new work, the *Cambridge History of the Bible* is in progress, volume two being published in 1970.

It was a somewhat crackbrained eighteenth-century bookseller, Alexander Cruden (1701–1770) who gave us his everlasting *Cruden's Concordance* (see Terminology, chapter 10), in 1737. Revised in many editions and under many imprints, the best modern revision is probably that done by Lutterworth Press, 1930, from £1·50 to £4·20 according to binding.

We may be asked, if we specialize in our stock, to supply a 'Harmony' of the gospels. This is an edition in which the four gospels are presented as one consecutive narrative. The scholarly term for such an edition is a *diatessaron* – a concord in four.

Many enjoy the Bible when it is arranged like, for example, *The Bible Designed to be Read as Literature* (Heinemann, 1937). The complete AV and the Apocrypha, 'designed for general reading' as *The Reader's Bible* (OUP, 1951, 1, 988 pp.) may be recommended with confidence to any interested customer.

Well-illustrated handbooks on the archaeology of the Bible attracted a popular market during the 1950's and 1960's, becoming basic stock items in all except the smallest shops, with Werner Keller's *The Bible As History* taking its place in Hodder's back list as a standard work.

Brief as this survey is, enough has been said here to make it clear to all students how very complicated the bibliography of the Bible is for the trade. Few booksellers are able to master the subject thoroughly, for every year produces new books on this inexhaustible subject, with its own terminology, and a list of 'untold' editions in a bewildering variety of sizes, format and bindings, ranging from the costliest lectern Bibles to the smallest Oxford 'Ruby' editions, and the white Bibles for brides.

Chapter 14
Dewey Classes: 300-400-500

Of these three main classes of DC the middle one, class 400, will here receive most attention, for it will no doubt be helpful if some description in detail is made of the various dictionaries to be found in stock in the largest bookshops. It is a subject upon which advice is often requested by customers before purchase, and few aspects of daily work are better publicity for bookselling than the ability to give accurate, knowledgeable guidance on certain classes of books widely differing in price, scope, function and quality.

But before proceeding to this interesting branch of stock, let us study a few standard books classified as social science, or sociology, as it is sometimes called, to the confusion in former days of worthy aldermen on town councils, for whom it was always associated with socialism, and therefore viewed with considerable suspicion when mentioned in library reports.

We may conveniently mention here the renowned *Annual Register of World Events*, first published in 1759, and lately, even available as a *Penguin*, a most remarkable tribute both to the reference work and to the two publishers concerned. Every student must make himself familiar with the contents of the work, often classed in libraries in 909, universal history. It must be remembered with that other famous annual, *The Statesman's Year Book*, packed with facts and figures; and no doubt many will also have handled the American *World Almanac and Book of Facts*, a sort of American counterpart to our familiar *Whitaker's Almanack*.

A unique work in its class, not so well known as it should be in Great Britain, is the *Encyclopaedia of the Social Sciences*, edited by Seligman and Johnson, with a popular edition in eight volumes (Collier-Macmillan, 1935). Library customers and colleges not able to afford the set may be interested in *A Dictionary of the Social Sciences*. The defect of encyclopaedic treatment of such vast scope is apparent: knowledge is therein congealed, imprisoned, and set in a dated mould, whereas in the twentieth century, our conceptions and ideas, the field of knowledge itself, are for ever on the move, changing overnight under the impact of nuclear science, the problems connected with the developing nations of Africa and the East, rapid telecommunications and revolutions. Like *Books in Print*, an encyclopaedia is out of date on the day of publication. Hence the usefulness of such periodical reference works as Keesing's *Contemporary Archives*, recording week by week the significant happenings in the world, registering the ever-changing winds of the world's politics. Nevertheless, it is convenient to have basic topics, history, relevant biographical material, and the principles of classical economics discussed by authorities, in one set of eight volumes for colleges and libraries.

In the same class division of 300 there are other general works, and near by, at 303, we may find on library shelves the 1970 *Modern Dictionary of Sociology*, by the Theodorsons, which is an American work published in Britain by Methuen. It is the type of reference work that the Americans do very thoroughly, and it is cited here because it provides us with an example of a subject dictionary, as distinct from a language dictionary, and a glossary of specialized terms. The compilers have defined in A–Z order all the words and phrases used in sociology, political science, economics, statistics, and other related topics, with cross-references. Nowadays we are sometimes puzzled by the new meanings and extensions of terms, given by workers in this field to older, traditional vocabularies. Here is the student's answer.

Associated examples to be remembered are the *Parliamentary Dictionary* by Hawtrey and Barclay, the third, 1970 edition of which was a revision of a standard work published by Butterworth; and the 1969 reprint of the first two volumes of a classic of 1898, in Pollock and Maitland's *History of English Law* (CUP). A new introduction with a bibliography further increase the value of this work of legal scholarship to students of the period before the reign of Edward I.

All important divisions in DC 300 seem to have attracted the compilation of dictionaries, glossaries and similar reference books. I have noted scores elsewhere,[1] but will cite only one other, because it is one of a famous, standard series: *Everyman's*

1. See *British Book News*, October 1968, pp. 723–727.

Dictionary of Economics, subtitled 'An Alphabetical Exposition of Economic Concepts and their Application' (Dent, 1965). This most useful deskbook includes biographical notes on famous economists.

Some of the acknowledged classics of social science have been epoch-making: Adam Smith on *The Nature and Causes of the Wealth of Nations* (1776, 1791); Malthus on *The Principles of Population* (1798, 1803); John Locke on *Civil Government* (1690) with its cogent argument against the divine right of kings; Lecky on *European Morals* (1869). Others, though minor, also deserve a place in *An English Library,* where they will be found on pages 222–248. Gustave Le Bon's *The Crowd* (1896, 1903) for example, was a striking forecast of the shape of things to come in the twentieth century, with its mass marketeering, mass-minded journalists, and the influence of the press generally; this interesting book may well be remembered with Trotter's discussion on *The Instincts of the Herd in Peace and War* (1916); while Veblen's *Theory of the Leisure Class* (1899) has had considerable influence on the political philosophy of the left wing.

Few general booksellers are able to stock books on economics, although the advent of *Papermacs, Unwin Books,* University paperbacks, added to *Penguins* and *Pelicans,* provide some of the standard monographs and students books. Only in the Economist's Bookshop attached to the LSE will perhaps the full range of stock be on display for the needs of students specializing in this and allied subjects, ranging from politics and philosophy to transport and education. Indeed their *General Catalogue of the Social Sciences* is itself a most useful comprehensive bibliography. The University of Oxford course known as PP and E (Philosophy, Politics and Economics) has produced for the Honours School an 82-page bibliography for students, to which interested booksellers may be referred. Those choosing the subject in the examination should mention it, and remember that Citizenship is a popular topic within class 300.

In this subject, at least, it is possible to mention books with a wider public than the academic, and to remember the several excellent introductions for young readers, especially *John Citizen,* by E. E. Reynolds. This was published in 1939 by CUP who have many notable books on economics and politics in their standard list and one would remember them along with

10

Allen and Unwin, Macmillan, and Routledge, as perhaps the most important publishers in this field.

When we proceed along the DC classes to 400, our main concern is with

Language Dictionaries

because all bookshops must carry a representative stock and the field of choice is unusually varied and wide. There are over a score of standard English dictionaries; nearly as many serving as ancillary compilations to the ordinary dictionaries, as well as many subject vocabularies. OUP alone have a distinguished list, and it is with their crowning achievement that we must start, not only because of its eminence as an example of the lexicographer's learning and skill, but because it is necessary to be aware of its bias and shortcomings. The great *Oxford English Dictionary*, 1884–1928, formerly known as Murray's Dictionary, because Sir James Augustus Henry Murray (1837–1915) was its chief editor, himself accomplished a prodigious amount of work on it for the Philological Society, and inspired a small, gifted team of devoted philologists who helped him to complete the vast undertaking in little over forty years, probably a world record for this class of dictionary. This 'New English Dictionary on Historical Principles' is in its present printing, a work of 13 volumes, royal quarto, 16,400 pages, including a supplement and a great bibliography of about 20,000 separate works used by the compilers to trace the first usage and developing meanings of words from the beginnings of English literature up to 1933 in the later volumes. Hence this dictionary is the most authoritative work of reference we have on the English language, and is used in law courts when the exact meaning of words is in dispute. The current price of the set (1972) being £90, limits its market to libraries, certain clubs, authors who can afford – and house – the great work, and universities. In 1971, however, a remarkable reprint of this vast work was made available in two micrographically printed volumes, at the astonishingly low price of £28 the set including a reading glass. This *Compact OED* has brought the complete work within the reach of almost every reader and student likely to be interested in it. But a language grows; its vocabulary changes by extension, addition and the lapse of certain meanings. Therefore great as it is, the OED has to be supplemented by smaller works kept in constant revision.

A modern supplement is in progress; hundreds of volunteers are preparing the word-index of twentieth-century English. Meanwhile, the smaller works of standing hold their own as up-to-date dictionaries. Moreover, the approach of the lexicographers to their work on the OED has always been a literary one, and hundreds of technical and semi-technical words, now in common use owing to the pervasive effects of technology and modern industrial development, the dissemination of knowledge to the masses by radio and television, and the popularity of scientific journalism, have found as yet no place in the dictionary.

Every bookseller will be familiar with the numerous offspring of OED, usually to be found in bookshops, especially the *Shorter Oxford English Dictionary*, now in its third revision, with corrections up to 1959, and available either in two volumes or in one thick quarto of 2,538 pp. For £6·75 this is undoubtedly one of the most desirable additions to all reference libraries, and one would like to see more offices and schools made aware of its superlative merits such as the retention from the parent work of many of the dated quotations in chronological order, revealing changes in meaning and stressing the correct use of words as exemplified by standard writers. Too often customers make do with the *Concise Oxford Dictionary of Current English*, adapted from the parent work, 5th edition 1964, 1,558 pp., £1·50. As its name implies, this is an attempt to provide a small dictionary of living English. The fifth revision was needed, for, compared with similar dictionaries, the COD lagged far behind in the inclusion of many words in common use. But the revising editor has now enlarged the vocabulary to provide definitions of older words that should have been in the earlier editions (such as euphoria, coronary, and many others) and of newcomers such as rat-race, ton-up boys, and feedback.

Before passing to dictionaries other than OUP publications we should note the latest *Oxford Illustrated Dictionary* (OID) which, as a quarto of 992 pp., published in 1962, £3, is rather more than its title indicates. It is virtually an encyclopaedic dictionary, with about 1,700 drawings in three-columned text, and should be of considerable use to schools, offices, and to foreign readers of English. Nouns are defined as in the

COD; illustrations, spelling and pronunciation guidance are given; the additional material includes biographical entries, some historical events, and much other information. For example, the Braille alphabet for blind readers and the alphabet for the deaf and dumb – these and other features must be remembered.

The smaller Oxford dictionaries stemming from the COD are to be found in all bookshops, and need no comment here; but a word of warning may be necessary regarding the standard and very popular works by A. S. Hornby and his co-editors. These dictionaries, known as the *Advanced Learner's Dictionary of Current English*, and an *English Reader's Dictionary*, have been primarily compiled for foreign students. As such they may not always be in basic stock, but they should be remembered by those dealing with export trade, and in the many towns and cities where there are now so many men and women from foreign countries living and working in Great Britain.

Finally, Skeat's great *Etymological Dictionary*, 1910, £4·20, 824 pp., is, as its name implies, more for the scholar than the popular reader. There is, however, a *Concise Skeat*, and many reference libraries have this for use by those who wish to trace the formation and inflexions of words from their origins.

For many users, there is little doubt that the most notable American publication in the dictionary class is far more satisfactory than the OED and its offspring. Webster's *New International Dictionary*, in its third revised edition of 1962, is a substantial work in which the editors have well remembered the statement of old Noah Webster, the founder, who wrote in 1817, 'a living language must keep pace with improvements in knowledge and with the multiplication of ideas' (quoted on the prospectus). This too, is encyclopaedic in treatment, with 3,000 text illustrations. Its 2,720 pages contain upwards of 450,000 entries, and the last editors estimate their intake of new words, or new meanings evolved from old words, as no fewer than 100,000; apart from detailed treatment of 5,000 synonyms. Webster has some other useful features, much appreciated by editors, writers, journalists and printers, especially those without a house style handbook: namely, the sections providing guidance on capitals and italics, forms of address, punctuation, the plurals of awkward words. Definitions include some sources of usage, and brief sentences illustrating correct employment of words, but slang is not disregarded, if well established.

The firm of G. Bell and Sons, which publishes this excellent work in Great Britain, price £21, reported a most satisfactory response to their 1962 edition, and I have heard a practised journalist declare that he would rather have it near his desk than any other dictionary of the English language. Like OID, Webster is encyclopaedic, for it contains a biographical dictionary, has a section on foreign words and phrases, and includes a world gazetteer. Based on this great work, we have Webster's *New Collegiate Dictionary*, which also includes the biographical section and the gazetteer. It was revised in 1963, and in its thin-paper format of 1,220 pp., is good value for £3·15.

In the same class, and from the same country, a comparatively new work known as the *Random House Dictionary of the English Language* is distributed in Britain by Collins, £10·50. In just over 2,000 pages the lexicographers deal here with 260,000 entries. There are 2,000 illustrations and maps, with a 400-page supplement including a gazetteer and atlas, and four bilingual foreign language supplements.

Wyld's *Universal English Dictionary*, Routledge, 1952, £3, 1,447 pp., quarto, is a remarkable piece of work by a learned etymologist, notable for its emphasis on the history of words. From this dictionary we pass to the smaller standard compilations, of which the most popular are Cassell's, with several offspring; Nuttall's, well established as a household book; Chambers's, much used by crossword solvers, and in its latest revision as the *Twentieth Century Dictionary* attracting great praise for its inclusion of technical, scientific and current words in general use. Annandale, Collins, Blackie: all of these are famous names in this field, and offer the most modest user extraordinary value for as little as 25–30p. In passing one may pay a tribute to Collins for their whole series of *Gem* dictionaries for French, Russian, Italian, German, Spanish, as well as English and Latin, all costing only 25p. each.

All booksellers should make themselves familiar with at least half-a-dozen of the new dictionaries specially compiled for children, especially the standard *Thorndike Junior*, revised for British children, and published by University of London Press. *Kingsway* dictionary published by Evans, is used widely in schools, especially the upper forms of junior schools, and from 1970 it has been available in an illustrated edition.

Before leaving this interesting section of book stock knowledge, we should consider a few standard dictionaries which are ancillary to the ordinary language dictionaries, noting the various functions they fulfil, and remembering them in daily work, especially if our own stock is not able to display more than a small section. Here indeed, it is most useful for our customers, with their varied needs and requests, if we are familiar with the books we do not stock.

How many assistants, for example, know that *English Idioms and How to Use Them*, by William McMordie, OUP, 75p (paperback 50p) has no equal in its class? I see from the third edition, revised in 1954, by R. C. Goffin, formerly of the Indian Educational Service, that it was 'written originally for students of the subcontinent now divided into India and Pakistan'. Its value to some great city populations in contemporary Britain should be remembered. It is an uncommonly well-arranged, systematic treatment of current usage. The second edition of 1913 was reprinted no fewer than twenty-one times. Here, then, is one of these best-sellers seldom mentioned in the trade or out of it, but yet quietly doing valuable work because it exactly and efficiently meets a permanent demand from every generation of students of English. Only those who have used it constantly know what a treasure the book is. And writing of treasures takes us at once to Roget's *Thesaurus* (a term that generically may be applied to a lexicon and a dictionary, and specifically means a treasure place or store), compiled by Dr Peter Mark Roget, and first published for him in 1852 by Longmans, Brown, Green and Longman. The present firm of Longman had the honour and pleasure of publishing the centenary edition, revised by two other Rogets, and the later, revised and enlarged edition.

Briefly, Roget's *Thesaurus* is a classified, systematic dictionary of synonyms and antonyms. But so skilfully has it been compiled, with such anticipation of the millions of different combinations of words, and with such understanding of the unnumbered correlations of human ideas and expressions which the English language is able to present in such diverse forms and shades of meaning, that the work is used by virtually all writers as not only a word-finder, but as a mental stimulant for the development of ideas. In addition to the standard Roget, enlarged edition Longman, 1962, £1.50, there are other works similarly compiled, presenting the same sort of verbal aid in varying degrees of thoroughness, including a new *International Thesaurus* from America, published in an English edition by Collins, 1963, £1·25. This modernized Roget deals with a quarter of a million words and phrases, and is praised in the country of its origin for the attention the editorial team has given to modern technical and scientific vocabularies. That feature must be remembered. It is the chief justification for the new edition. Remember, too, the distinctive features of *Everyman's English Pronouncing Dictionary*, by Daniel Jones, Dent, twelfth edition, 1963, £1·25, for this standard work lists about 58,000 words in International Phonetic Transcription; it does not define words. Its value to foreign users will be clear to all students.

Robert H. Hill's *Dictionary of Difficult Words*, Hutchinson, revised 1958, £1·25, and sometimes available in paperback format, is a useful work for students. There is Webster's *New Dictionary of Synonyms*, emphasizing analogues and contrasted words as well as straightforward antonyms in near 1,000 quarto pages, Bell, £5·25; and a well-known standard work in the same field of word study is Crabb's *English Synonyms*. An important newcomer is the 1970 publication of Cassell's *Modern Guide to Synonyms and Related Words*. Here the compiler deals with 6,000 words in just over 700 pages (Cassell, £3·15).

Almost every reader will have some knowledge of Fowler's *Dictionary of Modern English Usage* (OUP, 1926, revised by Sir Ernest Gowers, 1965, 725 pp. £1·40), although I have met people working in palatial offices, for wealthy firms, arguing about elementary questions of diction and grammar, completely in ignorance of the fact that their thinking had been done for them by H. W. Fowler, with far more authority behind his opinions and rulings than, for example, those of a young typist fresh from commercial school, upon whose verdict the decision to timidly split, or not to split, an infinitive verb, would be taken by experienced clerks. Who's Fowler? was the question. Well, let booksellers continue their good work in their respective communities, and Fowler may yet rival Culbertson and Hoyle in their ubiquity in office blocks of the twentieth-century postwar cities of Great Britain. We all have a long way to go if we are to get good books into offices as the essential tools that they are.

I may be unlucky, but in the same month which brought me into contact with a Fowlerless firm, I was asked by an expensively educated business man if Jane Austen was the title of a book or the name of an author. I told him of the village shopkeeper at Chawton, Hampshire, who, tiring of the constant enquiries made at his shop, by callers who never bought a thing, for directions to Jane Austen's house, had a notice placed outside with a hand pointing in the right direction: 'To Jane Austen's House'. But after a year he had to remove the board, because he was continually being pestered by callers, who never bought a thing, but asked if he would be so good as to tell them 'Who was Jane Austen?' *My* enquirer, who likewise, never bought a thing, merely looked at me with a pained, suspicious expression, because he thought I was enjoying a joke at his expense.

But with this digression, and reminder of this special type of dictionary compiled by H. W. Fowler to help writers, journalists and all of us, to avoid solecisms, errors, illogicalities in the use of the English language, and slipshod diction, we must leave that section of the average bookshop headed 'Dictionaries and Word Books'. After a year or two of experience, one would certainly expect all bookshop assistants to know much more than the range of English dictionaries. Some diploma examination questions, for example, have been framed to test the candidate's knowledge of the great standard works dealing with French, German, Spanish and Italian. Specialists have been exceptionally well served by R. L. Collison, whose standard bibliographical guide to *Dictionaries of Foreign Languages* is indispensable. Here it will suffice if mere key-names are given as pointers. Thus for the French language we should remember Larousse; Harrap; Cassell; Gasc and Chevalley. For German, Duden; Bithell; Cassell; Harrap; Muret-Sanders; Brockhaus; Langenscheidt; Bellows. Current editions of all of these dictionaries should be looked up in *Books in Print*.

For Spanish, check the latest editions of Cassell's, Harrap's and Routledge's, and give special attention to Holt's new work published by A. and C. Black and the 1971 Collins work. Many business students of Spanish as spoken in Latin America rely on the standard Appleton-Century dictionary.

The Italian language is now superlatively well served in a

great new work published in two volumes by CUP. Smaller dictionaries will be found in Allen and Unwin's list; Cassell's catalogue includes a standard Italian dictionary; and CUP also publish a well-known work by Hoare for those who do not require the larger Cambridge dictionary. With the publication in 1971 of the second volume of the handsome quartos of the new Sansoni-Harrap *Italian and English Dictionary* part one, the Italian-English section, was completed; £17 each volume.

From this brief remembrancer it will be obvious that publishers to memorize in this class of reference books are Cassell, CUP, Harrap, and Routledge. But we should not overlook Collins's *Gem* series of pocket dictionaries, of especial value to travellers. One final point to emphasize is that Cassell's *German Dictionary*, 1957 edition, was for the first time set in Roman, not Gothic type, thus helping students considerably in their quick search for words.

Harrap's *Standard French and English Dictionary* should be known as a stock title in most shops, as well as the *Shorter Dictionary*.

When recommending foreign language dictionaries one must be careful to ascertain the exact requirements of the customer, especially the grade of dictionary. That is, does the enquirer want an advanced two-way dictionary or a more simple vocabulary for beginners? Remember, too, that the *Concise Oxford French Dictionary* (sometimes known as Chevalley's) is a French-English dictionary only. The complementary work for English-French is by Goodridge. These two books are also published in one volume. Again: the famous and very popular *Larousse Dictionnaire Illustré* is what the title implies: a dictionary of the French language, wholly in French. *Liddell's Lexicon* is a Greek-English dictionary; *The Oxford Dictionary of Modern Greek* is Greek-English; but Swanson's *Vocabulary of Modern Spoken Greek* is a two-way wordlist: English-Greek; Greek-English.

The great new Harrap's *Standard German and English Dictionary*, now in progress, is in its German-English stage, which will run to four volumes, volume three appearing in 1971. In Harrap's special list, make yourself familiar with the Duden series; and the *Grosse Duden-Lexicon*, a truly great example of specialized lexicography, which when complete, in eight volumes, will have about 10,000 illustrations in text, plus 1,000 full-colour plates and maps. Library customers can often be persuaded to add such masterpieces, expensive as they must be, to the public reference collections for which they are responsible.

To end this section I will call attention to the invaluable *Guide to the Languages of Europe*, by Sir Archibald Lyall, Sidgwick and Jackson, 1932, revised and frequently reprinted. This is a phrase book with vocabularies in English and twenty-five other languages of Europe, with Arabic, Greek, and Esperanto, and a guide to pronunciation. Originally compiled for foreign office staff and embassy officials, Lyall's *Guide* is firmly established as a godsend to tourists and business men.

On the side lines are stacked such useful miscellanea as an *Abbreviations Dictionary* by Ralph de Sola (Constable, 1969), which is an international list of abbreviations, acronyms (see p. 92), anonyms, contractions, initials, nicknames, slang shortcuts, signs, symbols, and other fearful impedimenta of the contemporary struggle to survive, all arranged under fifteen headings, and printed in treble columns. Nothing comparable to this work is, so far as I know, available in any other language.

Then in the same year (1969) Warne's added to their popular dictionaries and reference works, a most unusual dictionary to be known for evermore as *Payton's Proper Names*. Students who are asked to describe *Payton* may be recommended to say that it is a new type of dictionary, being a vocabulary of words in fairly common usage today in English which are proper names, and which are therefore usually excluded from ordinary language dictionaries. Examples: *National Sporting Club* (1891), a London club which . . . etc.; *Venta Belgarum*, the Roman name for Winchester; and so on. Obviously Payton has come to stay, although I must state that Webster has always helped us by the inclusion of such proper names (and phrases compiled from them) as *Grand Lama* (which I could not trace in Payton) ; and *Exeter Hall* is even in cod.

Eric Partridge is a great name in unusual lexicography, especially famous for his work on Shakespeare's vast vocabulary, and for the great *Dictionary of Slang and Unconventional English* (about 2,500 quarto pages) published by Routledge. An enlarged edition of volume two of the Supplement was published in 1970, proving a further fascinating collection of 'colloquialisms and catch-phrases, solecisms and catachreses,[2] nicknames,

2. Examples of the improper use of words.

vulgarisms and such Americanisms as have been naturalized'.

Little known to booksellers, but worthy of support from schools and universities is the *Master Catalogue Series* (Morgan Grampian Educational) which has an unusually valuable guide through the maze of graded courses, readers, grammars and language books in *Modern Languages* compiled by B. C. Goodger (1967, £2·50).

Our next DC main class (500: Science) presents considerable difficulties to all booksellers, even the largest. Apart from the flood of popularizations of scientific subjects, much depends on the local industries and on the type of community served.

Nevertheless, students must acquire a working knowledge of the

Standard Reference Books in Science

of the type normally to be found in the average public reference library. Of these one may well start with Chambers's *Dictionary of Scientists*, revised 1961, £1·25, which would usually be classified at 925, but may be mentioned here as a standard example of a biographical dictionary related to a general subject. Chambers's *Mineralogical Dictionary*, 1946, £1·05, provides us with an example of a specific subject dictionary, in which the handy quick-reference form of dictionary has been successfully adopted to present scientific information on chemical composition, crystal form, properties, uses, and about 1,400 definitions belonging to the science of mineralogy. The latest additions to Chambers's list are a *Dictionary of Electronics and Nucleonics*, 1971, £4.50, and a new *Dictionary of Science and Techonology*, 1971, £6.50, described in the next chapter.

If we go through the main subjects of class 500 we shall see that many of them have this type of reference book. Thus for 520 (astronomy) we would remember *Larousse Encyclopaedia of Astronomy*, which in its English version, lavishly illustrated, has been a popular work in most bookshops, Paul Hamlyn, 1959. Astronomy is a subject which might well be chosen by a student with personal interest in the vast literature now available, in that it offers scope for the listing of key books for amateurs, beginners, and young astronomers, together with a few monographs on specific topics such as the stars, the sun, the moon, and space travel.

In James S. Pickering's *One Thousand and One Questions Answered About Astronomy* (Lutterworth Press, 3rd revised edition, 1969, £1·75) we have the most popular reference work in its class, worth memorizing even if it cannot be regarded as basic stock, as that perennial bestseller *The Concise British Flora in Colour*, by W. Keble Martin undoubtedly is (Ebury Press and Michael Joseph, £2·50).

Every shop takes a selection of the ubiquitous *Observer* book series on popular scientific, technical and natural history subjects. Like the *Ladybird* books for young children this series has made publishing history and, together, they are wonderful examples of British publishing for a world-wide popular market at almost 'giveaway' prices.

In classes 500 and 600 nearly all of us require the help of dictionaries of scientific and technical terminology. Flood and West's *Explaining and Pronouncing Dictionary of Scientific and Technical Words* (Longman) has already been mentioned as useful; W. E. Flood's *Scientific Words* (Oldbourne, *c.* 1963 – undated in publisher's list); Chatto's *Modern Science Dictionary*, 1961; and *Compact Science Dictionary*, by G. E. Speck, revised 1968 by Bernard Jaffe for addition to *Pan Books*, may also be recommended.

Why should the layman tradesman have to bother about this evergrowing jargon and nest of neologisms? Because before we are able to trace suitable books on certain subjects, we find it necessary to know what we are looking for. Only then do we know where to look, or how to take a short cut to knowledge.

If the trade searcher is asked for details of standard books on mutation, ethnology, anthropology, limnology, mycology, ecology, ontology, taxonomic botany and zoology, palaeontology, geodesy, topology, Laplace transforms, to quote a few requests, made during the actual work of an export office in the space of one typical month, it is not only educative, but almost imperative that he or she should know what these terms mean, especially if, like the present writer, he understands sympathetically what Charles Lamb meant when he wrote: 'In everything that relates to science, I am a whole encyclopaedia behind the rest of the world.' So look up the unfamiliar words in Flood and West; find out also the meanings of literary titles if you do not understand them. To sell Kinglake's masterpiece *Eothen* without knowing why it is so called is not good tradesmanship. Moreover, when one has looked up this word in the *Oxford Companion to English Literature*, the information gained may lead us to the reading, as well as the selling, of one of the most delightful early Victorian books in its small class.[3]

Terminology as used in modern science and technical literature helps one to use DC quickly. The knowledge may be superficial, but it is sufficient. Certainly we must not, as observed by Swift in the salutary *A Tale of a Tub*, serve books, 'as some Men do Lords, learn their Titles exactly, and then brag of their Acquaintance', yet the elementary knowledge accumulated merely by working with books we can never hope to read, or even to understand beyond the exact meaning of their titles, is not to be despised, because it does help us towards a higher standard of service. For even the full use of a catalogue of scientific and technical books, learned and academic books, is scarcely to be attained without this grounding, especially if the publishers have been thorough enough to catalogue, classify and annotate their books methodically.

Terms such as morphology, ecology, demographic, and the rest, may be special vocabulary, but that is one reason for our concern with them, for as we live and work in the vast world of books, many of our customers are scientific and technical workers, and pay us the compliment of expecting us to speak their own language. Moreover, occasionally, as with ecology, a scientist's terms will suddenly be on everybody's lips and in general use even in the popular press.

Returning to the study of class 500, wherein so many of these terms will be commonly found, remember certain series consisting of monographs serving both the trained scientist and the educated layman. Postwar publishing in Great Britain and Europe, the USA and Russia, is notable for its achievements in this class of specialist authorship. In British publishing, one would quote but two outstanding examples out of scores: the highly-praised Collins series, the *New Naturalist Library*, and Eyre and Spottiswoode's *Kew Series*. Each monograph is the work of an authority, and so well produced by the publishers that the average customer cannot help being attracted to subjects that interest him. In the same

3. For a full bibliography of technical and scientific subject dictionaries and glossaries, see my articles in *British Book News*, October–December, 1968.

category are Collins's *Pocket Guides*, these having attained the status of household books in a decade.

Apart from such standard, semi-popular yet authoritative books on scientific subjects, and the many introductions, there are few, if any, specialized books in 500 which would be regarded as basic or normal stock titles, even by the larger, general booksellers, other than those in university towns and cities.

The British edition of a popular one-volume *Encyclopaedia of the Sciences* (Allen and Unwin, 1969, £3·50) must be something of a treasure for schools and colleges, but once the obvious market is served, it may be difficult to sell to the general scientific reader.

There are no set rules to guide us, except those which govern our own business. An erudite, handsome, illustrated and authoritative work such as *Science in History*, by J. D. Bernal, 4 volumes, illustrated, in slip-case, is not dear for £10 (C. A. Watts, 3rd edition, 1965–1969); but when at the same time this work appeared as an unusual paperback bargain in the *Pelican* series (4 vols. £1 each) a whole new market was opened up. We take these things for granted too much, yet they are great cultural events for which our age may be remembered.

Chapter 15
Dewey Classes: 600–700–800

In order to keep abreast of current literature in applied science subscription to certain specialized bibliographies is necessary. Of these the most useful is the ASLIB *Book-list*, a monthly list of recommended scientific and technical books with annotations (62½p monthly). The Association of Special Libraries and Information Bureaux (ASLIB) serves industry, scientific libraries, and the staff of research and manufacturing firms. Its function includes the retrieval of information by the latest methods, documentation, and technical bibliography. Entries in the monthly list have a running number, like those in BNB, but the books listed are classified by UDC, because of the need for highly specialized, specific placings. UDC is also used in the catalogue of the Institution of Electrical Engineers, where a whole library is devoted to one subject, and the less-complex tables of DC would be imprecise. ASLIB *Directory* (of sources of information in Great Britain and Ireland) may be noted as an official guide in science, technology and commerce (2 vols., 1,018 pp. £6·30), kept up-to-date by amendments.

H. K. Lewis's catalogue has already been mentioned in chapter six. Do not overlook it when searching for books on applied science and medicine. The latter comes within DC 610–619 schedules. Before that we have placings for standard reference books on the whole range of technology, trades and manufactures in 600–699.

Continuing the theme introduced in the last chapter, the most obvious choice is Chambers's *Technical Dictionary*, followed by Oliver and Boyd's *Dictionary of Scientific Terms*; not forgetting the unique and very useful *Science Dictionary in Basic English* (Evans, 1965, £1·75). More than 25,000 words and word groups are defined within the limits of Basic English, that is, of the 850 key-idea words: a remarkable achievement.

A work complementary to Chambers's *Technical Dictionary*, and largely superseding it, was published in 1971 as *Dictionary of Science and Technology*, £6·50. Here the scope of the earlier book has been greatly increased to cover definitions of terms used in more than a hundred subjects. This will find a place in every public reference library and in the libraries of industrial and scientific concerns.

Technical Dictionaries at 603; foreign and polyglot dictionaries dealing with various branches of technology: these are highly specialized. Information about the available volumes has to be gathered from many sources, but the Collison bibliography and the catalogue of the specialist booksellers, Bailey Bros., and Swinfen, are the chief aids. For business directories, of which there are hundreds, the bookseller cannot do better than to obtain a copy of the very comprehensive catalogue of that section of the Commercial Reference Library, Guildhall, City of London. It is the best collection in range in London, and has few equals in Great Britain even in the largest cities of the Midlands and the north.

An exercise to be recommended is to select a subject, and then to jot down in not more than five minutes the names of publishers specializing in it. Thus every bookseller should be able to name without hesitation at least six publishers with medical books listed in special catalogues. They form the basis of all buying lists. Differentiate between books for professional nurses and those for use in the home. Usually books for the layman are classified at 649, with decimal point subdivisions.

Leaving these groups, and skipping engineering in all its branches because such subjects depend for their representation in everyday stock entirely on the locality and type of trade, we will turn to 630, where we find the standard books on

Agriculture

Here terminology is comparatively limited, but it is well to appreciate the differences between agriculture, horticulture, agronomy, farming. Each has its famous, standard books; most booksellers decide they can stock such classics as Fream's *Elements of Agriculture*, Murray, £1·50. Now in its 14th revised edition, it is the standard textbook prepared under the authority of the Royal Agricultural Society. Similarly Sir James Watson's *Agriculture: the science and practice of British Farming*, Oliver and Boyd, £3, is always kept up-to-date by

revision, and is now nearly 1,000 pages in length. The popular
work by James Gunston, the *Farmers' and Farm Students' Handbook*, Odhams Press, 1955, £1·05, is a suitable stock title for
many shops. I have found considerable interest in a list on
farming for young farmers, which includes not only the popular
series of handbooks on specific topics, published by Evans for
the Young Farmers' Club, but career books on a life on the
land and such simple introductions as *Farm Machinery Works
Like This*, by S. D. Kneebone, Phoenix House, 1963. One can
supplement this with a useful list for teachers on School
Gardening. Tropical Agriculture and Tropical Gardening also
attract numerous enquiries. As with others in the series, the
new *Oxford Book of Food Plants* (OUP, 1969, £2·75) attracts both
the general and the specialist reader.

More popular is the type of book intended for those who live
in the country rather than those who work in it. These books
usually are grouped at 630:1 Country Life. The witty Sydney
Smith had no relish for the country: for him it was 'a kind of
healthy grave'. 'In the country,' he wrote, 'I always fear that
creation will end before teatime.' But his quiet country rectories
and villages, and his leisurely London, are not ours, and most
of the pleasant books we find to make up a popular booklist
are for those who enjoy the best of both, such as they are in
this noisy age of motor car and jet. The delightful *Shell Country
Book*, by Geoffrey Grigson, and its successors quickly attracted
a sale placing them within the bestseller class. Of the earlier
books on my own Country Life list, I remember with affection
the simple, sweet-toned books of Alison Uttley (Faber), John
Moore's *Portrait of Elmbury* (Collins), H. E. Bates's *The Country
Heart* (Michael Joseph) and two books by Walter Rose, *Good
Neighbours*, and *The Village Carpenter*, both CUP. These two are
likely to be elected to the classic group, to keep company with
George Sturt's *Change in the Village* (Duckworth) and Thomas
Hennell's *Change on the Farm* (CUP). Hennell and Sturt have a
place in *An English Library*.

Midway in 600 we come to business subject groups, including
accountancy, auditing, packaging, advertisement, manage-
ment and related sub-topics; passing on the way the subjects
near to our own work: printing, book illustration, bookbinding, publishing and bookselling. Note the difference between
books at 651.02 (Secretarial Practice) and 347.72 (Company

Secretaryship). At 658.386 we place books on the use of films in industry, a new subject that has already attracted a dozen handbooks. Such a list is difficult to compile without a classified bibliography, since the subject embraces film animation, research films, film-making techniques, as well as the comprehensive scope of the principal handbook on *Industrial and Business Films*, published by Phoenix House, 1962.

One of the most recent imprints is *Business Books*. The current list must assuredly be attractive to every board room and company secretary's office, especially the 1970 *Businessman's Legal Lexicon*, and *Coping With Crime* (stealing, spying, fraud, tax, vehicles, race relations, and allied matters).

A satisfactory list may be compiled on the art of Chairmanship, 651.77, ranging from *Committees: How they Work*, by Edgar Anstey, Allen and Unwin, 1962 (now an Unwin paperback), to the same publisher's *Simple Guide to Committee Procedure*, 1924. From this group the remainder of 600 is devoted to Chemical Technology (660); the Food Trades; with Wine at 663.2. Cook Books are placed at 641.5. Both subjects lend themselves to selective treatment for examination purposes, because they have attracted such a great number of first-class books. If you decide to concentrate on national cook books, place them at 641.59 (note the mnemonic), and differentiate between books for the professional chef and the household. Here too, there is room for a separate list on quantity catering.

Concluding, one must remember that all DC classes from 500 to 699 are covered in Whitaker's *Technical Books in Print*, mentioned in an earlier chapter.

Traversing manufactures, textiles and woodwork, we come to the final group of ten from 690 onwards, dealing with subjects connected with Building Construction, Plumbing, House Decoration as a trade and craft, taking us into the next class, 700, reserved for the Fine Arts, Recreation, Games, and Sports.

The Fine Arts

from 700 to 789, are best approached by way of publishers' catalogues and the stock with which students are familiar. No group of subjects has attracted such a wealth of superbly produced and illustrated quartos. Many of these books have been so marketable that they have lent themselves to merchandising techniques, and are none the worse for that. They have put money in booksellers' tills; brought colour and beauty to shops, flats, houses and children's schools; freed thousands of people from the inferiority complex their parents used to have when confronted with anything more difficult than the pretty picture on a chocolate box; helped to create the inspiring queues one so often sees at art galleries.

Those who specialize in art subjects do so because they have personal interest in the folios and quartos, imported, or produced so magnificently in this country by Thames and Hudson, Oldbourne Press, Faber, André Deutsch, Weidenfeld and Nicolson, Phaidon Press, Phoenix House, Paul Hamlyn, Collins, Methuen and others from whom we expect such books, which we can stock with confidence.

At the one end of the working list we shall find the multi-volumed survey known as the *Encyclopaedia of World Art*, a truly imposing set of 15 quarto volumes, a 'summation of the visual arts of all times and places', published by McGraw-Hill, in collaboration with an Italian Institute at Rome. Volume 15 indexes the whole work, which has no fewer than 7,000 plates, of which 1,400 are in colour. This is a set for libraries. At the other end of the scale we have Thames and Hudson paperbacks, *Fontana* paperbacks, and Methuen's *Little Library of Art*. Truly this is a section of publishing that has made postwar history, with as yet unestimated cultural influence on the twentieth century.

The splendid quartos from Thames and Hudson: *Encyclopaedia of the Arts* (1966, £8·40); and the *Picture Encyclopaedia of Art* (1958, £4·75) may be known to those who work in the larger bookshops and to library booksellers, but smaller reference works worth memorizing are *Everyman's Dictionary of Pictorial Art* (2 volumes, Dent, 1962, £1·75 each); and the *Penguin Dictionary of Architecture* (1966, 42½p). The superbly illustrated *Glossary of Architecture, 850–1830*, by John Harris and Jill Lever (1966, Faber, £5·20 is also a Faber paperback, £1·25).

In 1970 OUP added an important illustrated volume of nearly 1,000 pages to a scholarly but popular series with the *Oxford Companion to Art* (£6); and earlier there was a welcome, revised edition of the *Oxford Companion to the Theatre* (1,104 pp., 80 plates, £4·20).

Do not overlook art appreciation for children. There are

Elizabeth Ripley's monographs published by OUP in the young people's section. Among standard series the *Oxford History of English Art* and the *Pelican History of Art* should be remembered.

At 708 we gather together Collectors' Manuals, general and specific, with a subsidiary list at 708.1 for reference books on Gold and Hall Marks, Pottery and Porcelain makers' marks. Books for architects go at 720; Handicrafts and Cottage Industries at 745, with subdivisions. This is a most popular booklist at home and abroad. Photography (770) attracts hundreds of books, and here the buyer, and the lister, has to exercise very careful selective flair. It is a subject lending itself to presentation for examination purposes, from the expensive reference books for professionals, to the most widely-used *All-in-One-Camera Book*, started in 1939, and now in its sixtieth edition. Certainly a remarkable bestseller in the Focal Press list. Beyond this subject, 770, we find music at 780, and then from 790 to the end, the group concerned with cricket, football, riding, swimming, yachting, angling, and field sports, combat sports, indoor games and pastimes. Here too, at 791.5 we have Puppetry (a good listing topic) and the Theatre (792), with the ever-popular Ballet as a subdivision at 792.8. In this rapid survey I have said nothing of the growing literature at 747.9 (Flower Arrangements and Floristry), nor of the collectors' and dealers' handbooks at 749.2 on Period Furniture. Learn their literature if you are interested and you happen to work in a shop where they can be featured as stock.

The Literature of Music

is a convenient and interesting demonstration of a method of dealing with examination questions demanding a knowledge of many books on one subject, selected to display the candidate's acquaintance with books of every type and form, from books intended for professional musicians, to those for skilled amateurs, concert-going music-lovers, Promenaders, young musicians, teachers, and schools. Hence the range will be from standard reference books to simple introductory primers, enabling students to exemplify knowledge of every category defined in chapter ten.

At the head of such a Music List, I suggest we place as a standard

Reference Work – Grove's Dictionary of Music and Musicians (1878–89) 5th revised edition, 10 vols., Macmillan, 1954–1961. £40 (the set).

It is the greatest work of its kind, and although the period when it was stocked has gone for most shops, it must never be forgotten when compiling buying lists for important customers and foreign libraries. Running it very closely is the more specialized

Cobbett's Cyclopaedic Survey of Chamber Music, 2 vols. OUP (1929), revised edition 3 vols., 1963, £12·60, 1,474 pp.

Popular reference works abound; and one would expect the *Oxford Companion to Music* to be on all lists, and to remind the compiler of the *Junior Companion*. I would not draw up even the smallest group of such books without giving therein a place to *Everyman's Dictionary of Music*; the *Concise Oxford Dictionary of Music*; Collins's *Music Encyclopaedia*; and Rupert Hughes's excellent *Music Lover's Encyclopaedia*. Davis's *Music Dictionary* is a first-class compilation published by Faber, for young musicians and schools; while Peter Gammond's *Terms Used in Music* (Phoenix House) is a useful glossary. In 1970 Harrap added a new *Opera Guide*, by Sir Alexander Morley (£2·50) to their reference list. One might finish this section with the popular Penguin *A New Dictionary of Music*, by Arthur Jacobs, and still have to omit several good books. What should be recommended as a

Monograph? – A classic example is *Alessandro Scarlatti: his Life and Work*, by E. J. Dent. Edward Arnold (1905), reprinted 1960, £1·50.

Next we should think of at least one textbook for students and professional musicians in training, and of the hundreds available, might choose as a well-known example on a specific topic

Textbook – Harmony: a textbook for class use, by A. O. Warburton, Longman, 1952, 85p

noting with appreciation the correct use of the term 'textbook'.

Musicologists appear to be more accurate and careful in this respect than many other authors. A critical, definitive edition of a

> *Classic – Dr Burney's Musical Tours in Europe*, edited by Percy A. Scholes, 2 vols., OUP, 1959

may be cited. First published in 1771. Dr Burney, Fanny Burney's father, achieves immortality for this amusing personal narrative rather than for his formal *History of Music* (1776–1789).

We may choose as a representative example of a

> *Handbook* – Eric Hope's *Handbook of Piano Playing*, Dennis Dobson, 1955, 55p

intended for students with some proficiency and knowledge. As an introduction to a comprehensive subject, one might list the attractively illustrated quarto by Benjamin Britten and Imogen Holst, *The Wonderful World of Music*, Macdonald, 1968, £1·05, because it is suitable for young music-lovers as well as adult listeners. Alternatively there is the standard, but much more advanced work by Professor David D. Boyden, *An Introduction to Music*, Faber, revised edition 1971, £5. This has a foreword by Percy A. Scholes.

Publishers' series abound, for music is a subject inviting monographs. Perhaps the most famous and well-established of all in this class is

> *The Master Musicians* series of monographs, edited by Sir Jack Westrup, Dent, 28 volumes, from 90p to £1·40 each.

These books reach a wide, popular audience, as well as students of music. Each is the work of an authoritative writer, who provides a biography in brief of the composer, followed by a detailed critical analysis of his music, with a bibliography and a complete list of works.

The above summary presents the subject of music fairly enough for students selecting it for an examination and requiring examples of the various kinds of treatment it demands from authors. Students should add to or vary the list according to their interest. Thus one could recommend as a well-known example of a popular handbook the perennial favourite edited by A. L. Bacharach, the *New Musical Companion*, Victor Gollancz, £1·05; and of the many good books for young music-lovers, Kitty Barne's *Listening to the Orchestra*, Dent, paperback edition, 37½p.

Music is so well represented in the *Oxford Catalogue* that we have to take care to avoid answering a question by citing only OUP publications. As we noted in a previous chapter, this pitfall (for such it is in an examination), is one to be avoided even more carefully when we deal with books in class 800

Literature

which, so far as the English classics are concerned I have dealt with in such detail in *An English Library* that I must refer readers to that Bookman's Guide for the essential information, especially pages 59–190 and 249–319. In the final section, *A Bookman's Reference Library*, pages 345–357, will be found details of the ready reference books likely to be needed by students. All that I propose to add here is to observe that DC 800–809 is reserved for general themes, including the formal treatment we find in the *Concise Encyclopaedia of Modern World Literature*, edited by Geoffrey Grigson, Hutchinson, 1963, £3·15; and the national treatment followed in the massive *Guide to Modern World Literature* (Wolfe Publishing, 1972, £5). American Literature is grouped at 810 (histories) up to 818 (American miscellany) leaving 819 for Canadian Literature. A reference work such as the *Dictionary of Fictional Characters*, compiled by William Freeman, Dent, £1·25, would be classified either at 803 or 823. It is a very useful addition to a bookman's reference library, helping to trace a character to its source in a novel.

From 820 (English Literature) onwards to the end, national numbers, characterized by the mnemonic mentioned in the chapter on DC, determine the order, plus subdivision by forms. These, for each national group, are: 1: Poetry; 2: Drama; 3: Fiction; 4: Essays and Belles Lettres; 5: Oratory; 6: Letters; 7: Satire and Humour; 8: Miscellany, with a group at 829 reserved for books in and on Old English (Anglo-Saxon) Literature.

There are a score of standard histories of English Literature
to choose from; one (the *Cambridge History*), being a collective
work in fifteen volumes, so termed because an editorial team
working under a general editor, developed the theme in detail;
another (the *Oxford History*) a series of twelve separate volumes,
each the work of one author; and the remainder varying from
students' *Introductions to English Literature*, edited by Bonamy
Dobrée, Cresset Press, 5 vols., now in both hardcover editions
and in students' popular paperbacks, 75p each, to popular
one-volume surveys, such as John Buchan's (Nelson).

Sir Paul Harvey's *Oxford Companion to English Literature* is a
basic stock item. It has been kept in revision by Dorothy Eagle.
The fourth edition has been enlarged to 972 pages (£2·50).
In 1970 a new edition of the *Concise Oxford Dictionary of English
Literature*, 608 pages, was published in hardcover format and
also as an Oxford paperback (£2 and £1 respectively).

There is a formal group classified at 808.88 relating to

Familiar Quotations and Phrases

requiring detailed attention here. We have an unusually varied
choice for stock, and an even greater one for that part of our
memory reserved for knowledge of books we do not stock. If
we are to advise customers wisely it is necessary to know as
much about quotation books as about dictionaries. Hence
whenever we get the chance we must examine the books and
try to memorize their special features, especially the arrangement of the passages quoted.

Characteristic arrangement may be alphabetical under the
authors, classified by subjects arranged alphabetically, chronological according to authors' dates and book dates or alphabetically according to the first purposive word. One of the
more costly, as well as most famous, is the *Familiar Quotations*,
compiled by John Bartlett, first published in 1855. Macmillan
published an enlarged and revised centenary edition in 1956,
with the 113,500 entries arranged in *chronological* order. This
great volume of 1,614 pages (£4·20) is too big for many users,
but it will be found in all but the smallest libraries. A smaller
volume, being a revision of the original in 524 pages, is done by
Routledge, £1·40. Bartlett described his work as 'an attempt
to trace to their sources, passages, phrases and proverbs in

common use'. Both editions preserve his *chronological* arrangement. Mnemonic: BC (Bartlett-Chronological).

Another costly reference work for library use is Burton
Stevenson's *Book of Quotations*, Cassell, 4th edition 1946, £8·75,
2,856 pp., quarto. Here the quotations are arranged alphabetically under *subjects*. Mnemonic: SS (Stevenson for Subjects).
Perhaps the most widely-used book of all in home and office,
library and board room, is the *Oxford Dictionary of Quotations*,
OUP, 2nd revised edition 1953, £2·50, 1,024 pp., quarto. This is
a reference book that may be read through from cover to cover,
for it is more in the nature of an anthology of great, famous,
wise, witty, and well-known passages, than a mere quotation
book. But note the arrangement well. Because of its nature and
its bias towards literary quotations, the passages are arranged
under *authors*, with index entries under key words. All quotation books depend on their indexes to make them serviceable as
quick reference books. These indexes obviously vary in nature
according to the arrangement of the main work. Familiarize
yourself with the additional features: for example, the *Oxford*
has a special group of Bible Quotations; many from the Book
of Common Prayer; an unusually generous choice from
Shakespeare; and gives the original Greek, Latin, French,
German, etc., for foreign entries, as well as the English translations. See Oxford paperbacks for an abridged concise edition.

A newcomer is the *Penguin Dictionary of Quotations*, compiled
by J. M. and M. J. Cohen, available in the library, cloth-
bound edition of 664 pp., published in 1962 by Cape, £2·10.
Here too, author arrangement has been adopted, with a
generous selection of French quotations; similarly, that other
newcomer, specializing in contemporary comments rather than
those with a traditional, literary flavour, Hyman's *Dictionary of
Famous Quotations*, Evans, 1969, £2·10, 516 pp., favours the
author arrangement.

A well-established household book is Sir Gurney Benham's
Book of Quotations, Proverbs, and Household Words, first published
1907, last revised 1948, Harrap, £2·10, 1,384 pp. Like most of
the books we have cited, British and American authors are
quoted, and Benham, too, chose author arrangement, with
subject index, differing slightly from Oxford's key word index,
although this obviously will sometimes also be the subject word.
Benham mingles with his subject headings a selection of first

or key words, thus getting the best of both styles. Benham is often the best buy because of its 150 double-column pages of proverbs, including those from six foreign languages; many users value it for its lengthy section captioned 'Waifs and Strays', being a group of odds and ends from the law, sundials, books, bells, epitaphs, the nursery, toasts, folk-lore, and countrymen's sayings about weather and crops, and so on, none of which can be attributed to an author. The work is especially strong on French, German, Italian, Spanish and Dutch quotations, with many from the Latin and Greek, each entry being given in the original, together with translations.

A *first word* arrangement may be seen in James Wood's *Nuttall Dictionary of Quotations*, last revised 1930, Warne, £1·50, 696 pp. But we must note the more usual author arrangement adopted in *Everyman's Dictionary of Quotations and Proverbs*, compiled by D. C. Browning, Dent, 1951, £1·25, 776 pp., with 6,000 quotations and 4,000 proverbs. A companion *Everyman* is devoted to *Shakespeare Quotations*, and we may note a single-source collection in *Biblical Quotations*, published by Elek in 1959. If we regard humour as a literary form, there are several anthologies of which the best are the *Treasury of Humorous Quotations*, edited by Evan Esar, Dent, 1958, which was added in 1962 to *Aldine* paperbacks; and the new Cassell's *Book of Humorous Quotations*, which is an American compilation in 436 pages of small quarto. Here is provided an index of key words, and the range is from BC to Churchill. All quotations are arranged A–Z by subject. (Cassell, 1970, £3.)

Finally, to conclude this survey of an interesting class of reference books, well worth memorizing, there is Brewer's *Dictionary of Phrase and Fable*, first published in 1870. This is a household reference book that has served generations. It gives the sources and the meanings of current phrases and allusions, such as, to cite only one example from thousands, the expression 'to curry favour'. We all know what this phrase means, but it is scarcely possible to understand its origin without the help of the indispensable Brewer. Such a book is therefore in a different category from the ordinary quotation compilations. It helps us to uncover layers of history, and by so doing, to reveal original meanings and the correct application of phrases in everyday use.

The standard revision of Brewer is now the completely revised centenary edition edited by Ivor H. Evans. Some outdated material has been deleted, so that the previous edition is still useful to students, but there is a much wider range of phrases culled from the Commonwealth and the USA, together with additional fable material from Wales and Ireland. It is a handsomely produced work, and in the words of its original compiler, Dr Ebenezer Cobham Brewer, is indeed 'an alms-basket of Common Phrases, Allusions, and Words which have a tale to tell' (Cassell, 1970, £3).

In this chapter I have omitted all mention of classic and standard fiction, because I have taken it for granted that students will have a detailed acquaintance with the three great series of classics: *Everyman's Library*; *Worlds Classics*; *Collins's Classics* (and the subsidiary series). All systems of stock control in every charter bookseller's shop must ensure that customers can be supplied from stock with the perennial bestsellers in these series: in fiction, poetry, drama, belles-lettres, history and other classes of creative and imaginative literature. Students will also be familiar with the inspiring range of great international literature in *Penguin Books*.

Special attention should be given to the OUP series, although not all of these are regarded as basic stock. *Oxford English Texts*, the companion and less expensive *Oxford Standard Authors*, *Oxford Paperbacks*, the recent series of *Oxford English Novels* in which scholarly texts are provided of many minor classics not available in other editions, and the series of reprints of foreign literature in English translation.

Chapter 16
Dewey Classes: 900–909; 920–929; 930–999

It will be remembered that the classifier derives DC numbers for Biographies and Autobiographies from the group at 920, adding to the first digits (deleting the final 0) the class number for the subject with which the person whose life story is being classified is connected. And that the travel numbers, including geography, are formed by inserting the digit '1' between the first two digits of the history national numbers. First we will deal with the literature of

History

beginning with 900 to 909, reserved as always, for general treatment of the subject. Hence 900 classes Universal History; 901, the Philosophy of History, and by extension, Civilization; while treatises on Historiography (that is, on the historian's art, the writing of history) are placed at 907. At 909 we classify comprehensive books recording modern world history, the term 'modern', here meaning the history of the world from the fall of Rome in AD 476. Twentieth-century history takes the decimal division 909.82. Ancient history (Greek and Roman) will be found at the 930–939 group; hence archaeology becomes 913, since it is the description and study of antiquities. It is at 901 that we would find the bestseller of 1969, Lord Clark's *Civilisation*, John Murray and the BBC, £4·20.

History books may mean to a bookseller, and a customer, school books; or the vast discussion to be studied in Toynbee's great work, now complete in *Oxford Paperbacks*. In between we have the classics, from the first Greek historians through the centuries to Gibbon's masterpiece, to Macaulay and others of the nineteenth century. The English classics are described in *An English Library*, pp. 191–221, including certain classic translations of Thucydides, Herodotus, Suetonius and other Greek and Latin works. G. M. Trevelyan's standard, popular

histories, his monographs on his special period, together with
the works of other twentieth-century historians, such as Sir
Lewis Namier, are also entered as they are no longer living. It
will be remembered that *An English Library* is limited by this
arbitrary but convenient rule.

There is a considerable corpus of contemporary historical
writing that should, and in most shops, does, form an
important section of displayed stock. These books are basic
stock. That is, by his stock control methods and records, the
bookseller establishes a routine to ensure that he is never without at least one copy.

The exercise suggested at the conclusion of this final chapter
indicates the sort of knowledge examination students should try
to acquire if they have not yet had enough practical experience
to enable them to accumulate it from their daily work in a
large bookshop. Here I would first emphasize the importance
of understanding the divisions of historical writing, because
the differences are so pronounced that books will be classified
in classes other than 900, even though they are histories. Thus
constitutional history is largely a matter of law. Hence the DC
number for the constitutional history of France will be, not
944, but 342.4 (300 – Political Science; 40 – Jurisprudence;
2 – Constitutional Law; 4 – national number: France). Political
History is classed in 300 (320) in some libraries; Military History
at 355.9; Economic History at 330, leaving formal history and
social history at 900.

Standard reference books should be remembered even if
they are not basic stock titles. Thus, consult in a public library
such works as Langer's *Encyclopaedia of World History*, Palmer's
Dictionary of Modern History, and *A New Dictionary of British
History* edited by S. H. Steinberg. The British edition of the
New Century Classical Handbook is published by Harrap; and the
Oxford Classical Dictionary (classed either at 870–880, or 900), a
large crown quarto of 1,120 pages, is indispensable for scholars
and students. Note that the 1970 edition revised has an index
of proper names (OUP, £6·30).

As in literature, there are examples of collective histories and
multi-volumed series, each the work of an authority on a given
period of history. The most famous collective history is the
Cambridge Modern History, planned by Lord Acton at the turn
of this century. His original work is now replaced by the *New*

Cambridge Modern History, completed in twelve volumes in 1970, £4 each volume. Of the other type, where each period is dealt with by a different author, there are several standard examples. To cite three: there is first the *Oxford History of England* series, from the Roman occupation to 1945. This, under the general editorship of Sir George Clark, is now complete in fifteen volumes. It may be remembered that the final volume, A. J. P. Taylor's *English History, 1914–1945*, took the trade by surprise. Within a few days of publication and initial reviews, it was on the bestseller lists and almost everybody was out of stock.

The second example is *Longman's History of England*, started in 1955 and in progress; and a third might be the well-known *History of Mediaeval and Modern Europe*, published in eight volumes by Methuen, whose back list has always been famous for scholarly historical works.

Of course, few except the university bookshops can carry a representative stock of such books, for the scope is wide, and includes new publishing ventures of spectacular magnitude, such as Weidenfeld and Nicolson's *History of Civilisation*, 1963– in progress; and the great *History of Mankind* (the Unesco enterprise in progress), by many distinguished authors, including Sir Leonard Woolley and Jacquetta Hawkes. These are historical writings on the grand scale, forming the mental background to the standard stock of the smallest bookshop.

Popular school histories abound. The pictorial histories by R J. Unstead (A. and C. Black) have sold by the hundred thousand, making publishing history for books in their class; the latest monographs for GCE students, the *Blandford History Series*, edited by R. W. Harris, Blandford Press, 1963–, are exemplary in clarity of presentation, and high standard of book production; the older Marten and Carter Histories, in four books, Blackwell, have held their own for generations; and *An Outline History of the World*, by H. A. Davies, OUP, 1954, £1·25, compresses the narrative into about 500 pages with remarkable skill. Paperback reprints of classics have brought scholarship and authority to the masses and to the personal libraries of undergraduates, who now need to borrow only the costly, many-volumed works, and source books, which form a class of their own in history.

One would expect all shops to stock Collins's first-class

Fontana History of Europe, the first to make an original appearance in paperback format. These specially commissioned monographs will deal in twelve volumes with the period from the close of the Middle Ages to the end of the second world war. They are addressed to the general reader and the student alike. In this notable series we have George Rudé's *Revolutionary Europe, 1783–1815*, especially valuable not only for the fluent narrative, to be read for enjoyment as well as study, but also for editorial attention to such details as maps of Europe in the period, a map of Paris in 1789, a list of a hundred books for further reading, and a most interesting glossary of French terms common in the revolutionary period, such as *assignat* (revolutionary paper money), *banalités* (which might well fox even an advanced student in an examination if compelled to make a guess of it), *corvée* (still in common usage, of course as a chore, a fatigue, but historically a peasant's obligation to do unpaid labour on the roads) . . . and so on. Truly, *Fontana* history is history without tears.

From Thames and Hudson we have in their *Library of Early Civilisation* a distinctive and quite unique series of scholarly paperbacks presenting ancient and classical history in text and in pictures. Thus *The Warring States of Greece* (to the Roman Conquest), by A. R. Burn, reproduces in colour plates, in pictures in the text and in line maps, hundreds of the archaeological specimens of Greek art we gaze at in Athens, Delphi and Olympia. Hence this is a series to be sold to the holiday tourist.

Dictionaries of Dates, or chronology, are useful for reference. *Newnes Dictionary of Dates and Anniversaries*, compiled by Robert Collison, Newnes, 1966, £1·75, is invaluable, and should be introduced to all educators, editors, journalists, librarians, speakers, writers and office managers.

Now well-established, with further instalments to come, are the *Chronology* volumes edited by Neville Williams of the Public Record Office in London. First to appear was his *Chronology of the Modern World*, being a dictionary of significant dates in politics, the arts and sciences and other fields including literature and the drama, from January 1763 to December 1964. The entries are grouped according to subject under alphabetic captions, with a double-column index of names and subjects facilitating quick reference (Barrie and Jenkins,

£3). The second instalment was a *Chronology of the Expanding World, 1492–1762* (Barrie and Jenkins, 1969, £3·50). The third volume dealing with the period AD 800 to 1491 will appear in 1972.

Still further indebted to Dent, students and scholars, librarians and teachers prize *Everyman's Dictionary of Dates*, now in its sixth edition by Audrey Butler (Dent, 1971, £1·25) that has many useful characteristics which should be discovered by booksellers by examination of the book itself. For example, short entries on specific subjects such as the Hanoverian Succession and the Declaration of Paris, mingle with long narratives on countries, especially the USSR and the USA, with classified entries where material is gathered under a single heading, such as Musical Composers, Sieges, etc., arranged alphabetically, with relevant dates. Such features are time-savers to journalists in a hurry.

The 1968 newcomer to this field was the admirably edited *Teach Yourself Encyclopaedia of Dates and Events* (EUP, £1·25). Its range is from 5000 BC to AD 1950, in one fat pocket volume. Each double-page spread lists the dates for events under four columns: History, Literature, Arts, Science, and the index lists people, places, subjects and books.

Of the standard social histories, everybody will be familiar with Trevelyan's work, and will notice that in such narratives the emphasis is on the life of the people, rather than on political and military aspects, although these must be treated, inasmuch as they affect our daily lives and work, our misfortunes, miseries, triumphs and prosperity. Of the newer histories (Green's pioneer work will be found in *An English Library*), I like and always recommend with confidence, *A History of the English People*, by R. J. Mitchell and M. D. R. Leys, Longman, 1950, now a *Pan Piper*. This illustrated volume, resulting from research into minute as well as greater aspects of life through the ages, draws upon a wide variety of sources, including newspapers, diaries, letters and commercial documents. One learns therefrom how men have shaved through the pre-Gillette and pre-electric centuries; what they ate, and when, for the very hours when dinner was taken have varied considerably, as readers of Jane Austen will remember; how much they were paid; who swept the chimneys – alas, a nineteenth-century chapter of callousness and shame until Sydney Smith lent his pen to reform – and similar topics which could scarcely find a place in a history concentrated on politics and diplomacy.

For the distinguished writings of great contemporary historians, which attract popularity and achieve the sort of sales usually associated with bestselling novels, students will consult their own stock, which they will know by heart. Some will perhaps find the history section of my *What Shall I Read Next?*, CUP, 1953, 75p, useful as a remembrancer. Here are given details and notes of the scholarly, yet popular books by C. V. Wedgwood, A. L. Rowse, Sir Arthur Bryant, Steven Runciman (his *A History of the Crusades* is a masterpiece and a modern classic), F. A. Simpson, J. M. Thompson and many others.

Before we leave history, a word about DC 940.5. Here are classed the thousands of books produced on subjects connected with World War II. To find our way quickly through the shelves of the vast library already accumulated from 1939 to date, and still growing, we must use a classified guide, because the subdivisions of 940.5 separate the phases, campaigns and regions of the conflict, enabling us to pin-point a topic, accumulate the literature on it, and to concentrate on a facet of this complex epoch of twentieth-century world history. Thus if we want to isolate the literature of submarine warfare, 1939–1945; or narratives of the war in Burma; or personal narratives of escapes; or air warfare; or diplomatic aspects; or official histories; or food control at home; or prisoners of war camps; or cabinet documents relating to Orders of Battle; or activities of the Polish Government in Exile in London, and so on, all we have to do is to ascertain the DC subdivision symbol for our topics, however minute, and at one glance the required items are located, brought to the surface from beneath layers of thousands of volumes that have submerged them. Sometimes the numbers may seem long and complicated, but this is not a drawback, and the building-up of those numbers is not our problem. If we find from BNB index that 940.54525(1) is the number allocated to Burma Campaign: Northern Kachin Levies: Personal Narratives, it will not take more than a few seconds to track down *The Hump*, by Jack Barnard, Souvenir Press, 1960, the only book on the subject, and one in which the title does not help the searcher at all. Logically we must now turn to

Geography

History is largely determined by geography, a subject that has become very specialized in the twentieth century. Now we have Human Geography (on the relationship of man to his environment); Commercial and Economic Geography (related to economic history, and dealing with trade and commerce); Political Geography (on the effects of geographical factors upon nations, boundaries and frontiers); Historical Geography (on the story of man's discovery of the earth he lives on, including exploration and material related to political geography); and Physical Geography (climate and descriptive geography, related, almost mingled with, the science of physiography, to be found at DC 551.4 because it is largely the description of natural phenomena). McGraw-Hill's *Illustrated World Geography*, 1960, £7, quarto, is one of the best modern reference books in the general class. I would expect any assistant with a little experience of books to say immediately Longman and Methuen, if they were asked to name two publishers famous for geography, for the greatest single name in geographical writing is that of Professor Sir Dudley Stamp, formerly Director of the World Land-Use Survey, and his many books on world and national geography are published by Longman, who also have in their list the standard Chisholm's *Handbook of Commercial Geography*, 18th edition by Sir Dudley Stamp (£5·50, 934 pp.).

Justly famous are Methuen's *Advanced Geographies* for honours students. Of the hundreds of school geographies, those to be found in the catalogue of the University of London Press should be familiar to students handling school authorities' bulk orders.

Finally, we may note that from 1970 the *Penguin Dictionary of Geography*, by W. G. Moore, is available in a hardcover library format from A. and C. Black, £1·50.

Atlases

It may be agreed that if one has to compile a buying list of atlases, an arrangement in price order is convenient, because this also arranges them in an order proceeding from the large, comprehensive library and board-room folios to the everyday home reference library atlases.

At the top of such a list, we would place the *Times Atlas*, in five folios, revised 1955–9, if it were still in print; but as it is not, in its place we put the current comprehensive one-folio edition, price £15·75, together with the *Times Atlas Index* mentioned below under Gazetteers (£10). *Atlas Général Larousse* (in Britain, from Harrap, 1960, £10), would follow.

Perhaps we come into the category of general stock when we reach the *Oxford Atlas* series, which must be known to every student by heart. George Philip and Son is also a famous imprint in the map and atlas world and Collins/Longman *Study Atlas*, 1958, should be included in school lists. The *Penguin* series of atlases, cheap, first-class and popular are in general stock.

In DC world atlases are classed at 912: national and local atlases (such as an atlas of London, for example) either at 912 (plus the national or local number), or at the national number plus the Dewey form symbol for atlases. Historical atlases usually go at 911, but some classifiers place them at the period number. Practice varies to suit the convenience of the library or list.

Thus, the new *Atlas of Great Britain*, a major work from OUP, 1963, £26·25, should be classified at 912.42. The *New Cambridge Modern History Atlas* (CUP, 1970, £8) could conveniently be classed with the impressive set of the completed work, which it crowns, at 909 or alternatively at 911.

Closely related to history and geography is a group of reference books and desk books known as

Gazetteers

so called because in the seventeenth and eighteenth centuries certain writers of official news-sheets, periodical publications called gazettes, giving a record of current events, movement of ships, and allied information essential to the merchant, were either supplied with, or compiled for their own reference, a kind of dictionary of place-names, with brief details, locations, and other relevant information. The *Shorter Oxford Dictionary* suggests derivation from the name (*gazett*) of a Venetian coin, that may have been the fee paid by those interested in the movement of shipping, people, etc., for a perusal of the news-sheet.

Modern gazetteers are dictionaries of geography, and some of them are so called. The characteristic arrangement of a

12*

gazetteer is alphabetical under place-names, countries and related topics. Information regarding population, trade, physical features, manufactures, etc., varies according to the scope of the volumes and the price. The *Times Atlas Index*, recently available (£10), is not a gazetteer but is more than a half-way house between a list of world place-names and a full dictionary of geography.

Gazetteers are seldom stocked, but as handbooks related to geography, are essential for libraries, schools, mercantile offices and official use. No doubt more could be done to increase the market for them. This then, is a class of reference book that must be known even if not stocked, and the most comprehensive work of its kind, an encyclopaedia of geography, should be remembered by every student. It is the great *Columbia Lippincott Gazetteer of the World*, 1952, £35·25, 3,158 pp., quarto. For ordinary library and board-room use one would recommend Webster's *Geographical Dictionary*, Bell, 1950, £6, 2,252 pp., 177 maps. This is a worthy companion to the biographical dictionary cited later. The handiest desk-book in this class is the well-known *Chambers's World Gazetteer and Geographical Dictionary*. A useful school book is *Philip's Handy Gazetteer*, to be used with the atlases. To be remembered when advising commercial firms stocking a working library for staff and executive use, is the unique Geographia's *Commercial Gazetteer of the British Isles*, 9th edition, 1956, £5·25 (slip case), packed with valuable information for sales managers, and Bartholomew's *Survey Gazetteer of the British Isles*, the 9th edition of which was reprinted in 1960, £3, 780 pp., quarto. One book on *The Rendering of Geographical Names*, by Marcel Aurousseau, Hutchinson, 1958, deserves special mention, as it is the only book I know on place-names in foreign languages, how to translate them for catalogues, gazetteers, and documents. The author, an expert on this unusual subject, has revised Lord Gleichen's unique book on *Alphabets of Foreign Languages*, Stanford, 1955.

As readers will have surmised, gazetteers take the DC number 910.3, a division of general geography. Guide books form a connected group of travel literature, stocked by all shops in season. Apart from Ordnance Survey Maps, few general bookshops carry much beyond the popular world maps issued by Stanford, the specialists, to whose shop we all go with admiration for their great collection, expertly filed and always in demand.

As far as the classics of travel are concerned, pages 320 to 346 of *An English Library* will probably provide all the information likely to be useful. Special treatment will be found, with bibliographies, in the Cresset Press series of *Introductions to English Literature*, mentioned in the previous chapter, of which volume V (the Present Age from 1920) should be consulted, together with the relevant section of *What Shall I Read Next?*, for contemporary travel literature.

Finally, to complete this rapid survey, let us pay some attention to that most popular form of current literature

Biography and Autobiography

The essay-introductions in *An English Library*, pages 15 to 58, with the details of the classics, will help readers to memorize the development of biographical writing from the earliest examples to our own time, and to understand the distinctions between various forms of autobiographical works, from diaries and journals, to the straightforward life-story self-told, and a volume of memoirs.

There are a few examples of modern collective biographies. These are listed in *An English Library*. Remember John Aubrey's *Brief Lives*, which, since the definitive edition and brilliant redaction by his biographer, O. L. Dick, has become very well known as a *Peregrine* paperback and on BBC Television and the stage. Batsford's *Historical Memoirs*, reprinted in paperback format, 90p each, is a series worth remembering.

Perhaps more than any other class in non-fiction biographies and diaries are subject to periods when they are in great demand, followed by a period of diminished public interest. In 1970 and 1971 an example of this occurred when Bell at last were able to announce the publication of the new, complete transcription of the *Diary of Samuel Pepys*, with full commentary by Robert Latham and William Matthews. This was an event of major literary importance, and for a time the demand for the first instalment of three volumes (£10·50 the set) was so great that many shops had a waiting list.

Further attention might here be given to Chambers's *Biographical Dictionary*, revised in 1968 (£4, 1,432 pp.). The best and most widely used desk-book in its class, Chambers gives a great deal of useful bibliographical data, and provides in the appendices information otherwise difficult to trace in this collected form. Thus, there is a subject index of 35 double-column pages enabling the searcher to consult the groups of famous people under the topics by which they are remembered. For example, under Literature and Drama we have an index of famous books and plays; under Art, a list of famous pictures, with names of the artists, and so on. There is also a useful list of nicknames.

For precise details of the *Dictionary of National Biography* (DNB) I would ask every student to consult the pages of the *Oxford General Catalogue*. Students' answers on this set of reference books are more often than not incorrect or too lacking in precise detail. No doubt all will be familiar with *Everyman's Dictionary of Literary Biography*. Include in the briefest survey such excellent junior series as Nelson's *Picture Biographies*; A. and C. Black's *Lives to Remember*; and the popular collective series for young readers published by Hamish Hamilton in which six great men and women connected with a single subject are chosen for collective treatment, thus contributing to the literature of the subject as well as to biography. The success of Thames and Hudson's series of *Pictorial Biographies* owes much to the choice of subject, the scholarly approach by authors who are able to write in a fluent style for the general reader, and above all, for the wide range of the 150 illustrations reproduced from many sources. This series may be recommended with confidence to schools as well as to the average customer. *Webster's Biographical Dictionary*, Bell, 1953, £5·25, 1,736 pp., is a well-established standard American work.

To help workers in special field and writers in an increasingly complex world, many subject biographical dictionaries are available. The latest, a *Biographical Dictionary of Scientists* (A. and C. Black) offers concise biographies of 900 scientists.

Due largely to the modern classics of Lytton Strachey, Hesketh Pearson, and Sir Harold Nicolson, biographical writing has attained a level of brilliant interpretation, wit, perception and liveliness that at once attracts the great public, and pleases the scholar. In this class twentieth-century literature is rich, as it is in historical writing, two forms closely related, and indeed relying on each other for material, for, as Carlyle observed in *Heroes and Hero-Worship*, 'The history of the world is but the biography of great men.' In his day, he could justly assert, as he did in his essay on Richter, that 'A well-written Life is almost as rare as a well-spent one.' He could scarcely know that his own life, written by his friend, J. A. Froude, would in 1884 usher in the modern art of biography.

In concluding this final chapter I realize that I have merely skimmed over the surface of a subject that must be a life-long quest for every bookseller – a knowledge of books of sufficient depth and of wide enough extension to enable us to offer the bookbuying public a service worthy of the world of books. But the foundations will have been laid. On them we can build upwards until we retire. None of us can hope to equal the standard set by the greatest bookseller-bookman of the century, the late John Wilson, C.B.E. I should have liked him to have written a foreword to this book, because he did so much to inspire and start the Booksellers Association in their education work.

It was John Wilson who first interested me in bookselling; it was he who started me on the lecturing activities for the BA that have resulted in *Bibliography in the Bookshop*. As Chairman and Managing Director of Edward Bumpus, Ltd., from 1941 to 1959, he could have looked down on all our efforts from a great height. He did not; he gave his time and energy to the scheme; found enough of both to devote evenings to attendance at lectures to satisfy himself that we were on the right lines; brought eminent authors with him to enrich those early Regent Street Polytechnic evenings; was active enough to the day of retirement to whisk one off to an evening meal after a tiring day in his busy shop and a perhaps, for him, tiresome attendance at a lecture dealing with elementary matters, and to talk throughout the session at his club – mainly about books. Before leaving his shop he would make sure on certain nights to have in his pocket a lump of sugar, saved from teatime in the poky little office, in order not to disappoint his favourite dray-horse usually to be seen in the neighbourhood.

Before one had been with him ten minutes he would be speaking of a new author who would be a coming man, or of a well-established author who had spent half-an-hour with him in that pocket-handkerchief of an office. It was not for nothing that when King George V was ill, he gave instructions for John Wilson, of Bumpus's bookshop, to be asked to send some books that he would enjoy.

And this great bookseller sent to Buckingham Palace exactly the right books for this occasion, as he would tell me with a shrewd, merry twinkle in his eyes: 'Sailors' yarns; old books; books by W. H. G. Kingston – *The Three Midshipmen*, you know.' These he knew the king had been fond of from youth upwards.

He once told me he would have liked to have been a librarian, 'and I think I'd have made a good one, too,' he added. Had he stayed in his native Glasgow I have little doubt he would have ended his career as a great Mitchell Librarian. But we in the book trade are glad he did not, and that he made the Scotsman's single trip to London when he was young. He should have written his *Bookshop Bibliography*.

If the educational work John Wilson did so much to start is to achieve the standard he set his heart on during the war period, the most important development of the 1970's must be a permanent School of Bookselling, where short residential courses will be available, and a permanent programme of lectures will be arranged annually.

Such a college, endowed, and well equipped with the tools of the trade, a booksellers' library, mechanical and technical teaching aids, a film theatre, and study rooms, might well be called the John Wilson School of Bookselling, attracting trained and untrained bookshop assistants, graduate and non-graduate beginners.

Appendix 1
Bibliography in Action

by F. Davids Thomsen, Managing Director of the Almqvist
and Wiksell Group of Booksellers, Stockholm, Sweden

Without any hesitation, I agree that bibliographical work forms the basis of all successful bookselling, although the efforts must needs vary considerably depending on the category of customers and the demand for bibliographical service in each bookshop.

Sweden may be taken as an example of a country with old book-selling traditions as a result of which there is today a network of well-stocked international bookshops in all the most important towns. The competition between the booksellers has forced them to provide an extensive bibliographical service to satisfy the demand of research and technical science for information, not only about national but, to a still higher degree, about international publications. Fortunately, research does not know of any boundary-lines and in Sweden, as well as in the other Scandinavian countries, an academic book, printed in English, German, or French, is just as welcome as if it were printed in the national language. Thus, it is a prerequisite condition for successful bibliographic work in an academic bookshop that all book publishing, throughout the world, be carefully watched. Although – to take an example – the main part of all books printed in English are published in Great Britain or the USA, a steadily increasing number of books, in all fields of research, are published in English in other countries as well.

In the present book, every available means of verifying material already printed is accounted for in detail, which is of invaluable help to the bookseller in solving the many problems, both simple and complicated, which he has to face in his daily work. By giving a brief description of the AW Documentation Centre which forms the backbone of the activities of the Almqvist & Wiksell Group of Booksellers, consisting of nine bookshops in five university towns in Central Sweden, I shall try to amplify the picture on two points, namely, as regards the furnishing of books in preparation with bibliographical data and, as regards the practical application, for promotional purposes, of the material collected.

Knowing that books in preparation, i.e. books which are still at a manuscript stage or in the press, very often are those most attractive to scientists and technologists as sources of information, the AW Documentation Centre carries out a continuous and consistent collection of information on books in preparation from all publishers of importance throughout the world who specialize – more or less – in the fields of Natural Science, Medicine, Technology, Social Sciences, and the Humanities, that is to say, in the fields where research-workers most keenly demand information.

The bibliographical data available about a book before it has been printed is naturally incomplete and approximate, both as to the number of pages and the published price, and sometimes even as regards the title, which may be changed in the course of printing, but from an information point of view this is not of vital importance to the reader seeking information.

Apart from the bibliographical data, a brief description of the content of the book is needed in order to enable the bookseller to make use of the material in the way described below.

The information received from the publishers gives evidence of numerous divergent interpretations of the conception Bibliography, but, fortunately, developments during the past few years show signs of definite improvement in this respect. Nevertheless, there are still many sinners! Elementary information, such as year of publication, author's initials, etc., is often left out. If omissions, for instance of the year of publication, are made on purpose to deceive the buyer, this must be regarded as a highly immoral act!

Advance information forms the basic material in the work of collecting bibliographical data, but in order to cover all subjects as completely as possible, it is supplemented by a thorough perusal of all current bibliographies, for instance, the weekly lists which appear in the *Bookseller, Publishers' Weekly* and similar publications throughout the world. The reading of these numerous periodicals is time-consuming, but worth the effort, since this is where we find, among other things, the important publications issued by learned societies, symposiums, etc. The advertisement and text pages also provide an abundance of useful information that, however, far too often suffers from a lack of complete bibliographical data and concise content descriptions.

The bibliographical and classified material thus retrieved now consists of information about books and new journals to be published, or just published, and this is registered on cards which, through a simple process, can be reproduced and distributed to the customers according to the golden rule that the bookseller's foremost duty is to bring the right book to the right man.

The subscribers to the AW Documentation Service comprise about 3,500 domestic customers of importance, namely public libraries, special libraries, university departments, professors, physicians, etc., etc., whose spheres of interest are carefully classified within approx. 140 subject groups. The subscribers are charged an annual fee of approx. £2·20 to cover postal expenses.

In order to give the reader some idea of the scope of our information service, I would like to mention that about 3·5 million information cards (see fig. 1) are produced per annum or, on an average, about 1,000 cards per customer. The number of titles covered by this documentation system amounts to approx. 1,000 per month. The distribution of the cards takes place twice monthly by means of punch card equipment which works in the following way.

For each subscriber there has been drawn up, on the one hand, a subscriber's card with information as to name, address, customer number and interests and, on the other hand, a subject card for each interest stated. With the help of the classification number on the original book card, the actual group of subject cards is extracted and in a 'reproducer' the customer number is transferred in punched form to the final information cards, which are then furnished with the text by simple duplicating. The subject cards immediately go back to the card index so as to be ready for use for the next title with the same classification number. The information cards are retained for further treatment every fortnight in a 'sorter', in which they are arranged by customer number together with a special address card, which in a 'translator' is furnished with the customer's name and address in block letters, transferred from the subscriber's punch-card. The address card of each customer is automatically placed at the top and consequently serves also as a marking-card. The information cards are now ready for dispatch and it only remains to insert them in window envelopes. As the card has our address on the back the recipient has only to indicate if the book in question is of such interest that it tempts him to a closer acquaintance, place a cross on the card, sign it and post it. It should be noted that most of the books included in our information system are offered to the customers on approval.

This is one of several ways in which a bookseller may activate his bibliographical work in order to promote sales. Since it involves rather difficult selection problems it is necessary that the task be handled by an experienced and specially trained staff and we, for our part, have entrusted the work to a highly qualified librarian whose task it is to find in this ever increasing flood of new books that very part of the production which is likely to interest an advanced group of customers.

On the whole, the selection and selling of scholarly and scientific books is much the same in bookshops all over the world and, as a consequence, the AW Documentation Centre has been able to establish close co-operation with a number of international book-sellers in, among other countries, Denmark, Finland, Norway, Germany, the Netherlands, Switzerland and New Zealand, who are able to make use of our editorial work for an annual charge.

Apart from its importance from the point of view of sales promotion, our bookshops have also, as a result of the system, obtained a bibliographical index which covers not only books already published, but also many books not yet printed. I hardly need point out what this means to the daily work in our bookshops. But, no matter how well a system works, there is always room for further improvements. The steady development of electronic data-processing and its increasing range of application also open up new prospects and possibilities for us which we are, at all times, prepared to look into and explore.

	AW:s Litteraturtjänst Gamla Brogatan 26 101 20 Stockholm 1 Tel. 08/23 79 90 erbjuder	**ALMQVIST & WIKSELL** 08/23 79 90
OBS! Ert abonnemang på AW's litteraturtjänst förutsätter att inköp av avise-rade böcker och tidskrifter sker i ALMQVIST & WIKSELL-företagens boklådor	Schoffeniels, E., ed. Biochemical Evolution and the Origin of Life (ISBN 0 7204 4084 X) (Molecular Evolution, Vol. 2) XII + 402 pp. 1971 North-Holland Ca. Kr. 140:- Contents: Allocution of Professor M. Welsch. Electronic factors in biochemical evolution — B. Pullman. The influence of the genetic code on protein evolution — J.L. King. Genes, chromosomes and molecular evolution — R.L. Watts. The neurohypophyseal hormones: an example of molecular evolution — R. Acher. Molecular expression of evolutionary phenomena in the primary and tertiary structures of cytochrome c — E. Margoliash. et al., etc. 23.4.71	**ECKERSTEINS** 031/17 11 00 **LINDSTÅHLS** 08/23 44 25 **LUNDEQUISTSKA** 018/13 98 30 **NORBLADS** 018/11 30 00 **SAHLSTRÖMS** 013/12 92 15 **SVENSONS** 018/13 47 06 **UNIVERSITETS BOKHANDELN** 08/23 12 90 **WESTLINGS** 019/11 90 20
ths = 288/368/7262	Reservation för ev. ändringar av pris och utgivningstid.	Glöm ej att fylla i namn och adress på kortets baksida.

Figure 1. Sample of information card
By simply cutting out the card along the lines indicated international standard size for library use may be obtained.

Appendix 2
Statement on the Service Basis Method of Charge

by the H. W. Wilson Company, New York[1]

Bibliographic publishing has always been a hazardous undertaking. The total number of possible purchasers is small, and the cost of production great, as compared with those for other types of publications. Furthermore, the publisher must be prepared to assume enormous risks for financing and carrying on a bibliographic enterprise during the necessarily long period while editorial work and printing are going on, for, until the publication is finally ready for delivery, no return on the investment is possible.

Records show that of hundreds of bibliographic ventures, most of them co-operative, not many have been financially successful. Of those mentioned in Jahr and Strohm's *Bibliography of Cooperative Cataloging* ... (Washington, D.C., Government Printing Office, 1903) only a few have survived. Most of them failed because the publishing agencies did not receive an adequate return for their efforts and not because the work was not needed or was not acceptably done.

It is customary when a worthy venture languishes for want of support to seek endowment or the aid of organizations willing to pay the deficit. Worthwhile enterprises are often helped to success by assistance of this kind. The H. W. Wilson Company, whose problem of financing its publications has been no exception to general experience, has devised, as a substitute for endowment, a plan which helps meet the difficulty and at the same time extends and strengthens a growing bibliographic system. This plan is the service basis method of charge, based on the principle that each subscriber should pay in proportion to the amount of service used.

Advantages of the Service Basis

The justice of this method of charging for bibliographic service is apparent. A library with a few readers, open only a part of the day, or a few days a week, naturally will not make the same use of

1. Reprinted by kind permission of the H. W. Wilson Company, New York.

periodical and book indexes that the large library does with its large staff, long hours, and many readers.

The service basis method of charge actually results in lower prices for all. If for the service basis plan we were to substitute a flat rate for all subscribers, many of the present subscribers would find their subscription rates increased so much that they could no longer afford to subscribe. The loss of their support would mean that the rate would again have to be raised for the remaining subscribers in order to meet the cost. This, in turn, would mean further discontinuances and further increases of rate until the time might arrive when only a few of the very largest libraries would be able to subscribe and at rates higher than they are now paying on the service basis.

The service basis method of charge enables each subscriber to pay only for the indexing he actually uses. It reduces the price to large libraries by enabling many smaller libraries to help pay publication costs; and at the same time it permits smaller libraries to have reference tools which they would be unable to afford at a flat rate which would necessarily be high.

How Rates Are Determined

The problem of how to determine fair service rates for all libraries was a difficult one, but the present system has developed gradually over a number of years. The H. W. Wilson Company indexes are divided into two classes – (1) the periodical indexes, where the subscription price is based on the periodicals that are indexed to which the library subscribes; and (2) the book indexes, including Cumulative Book Index, Book Review Digest, and similar tools, where the price is determined according to the library's book fund. For the benefit of the librarian who may like to know more definitely how these rates are applied, the following detailed description is given.

Periodical Indexes

Periodical indexes sold on the service basis include Applied Science & Technology Index, Art Index, Biological & Agricultural Index, Business Periodicals Index, Education Index, Index to Legal Periodicals, and Social Sciences & Humanities Index. The popularity of the periodicals covered by these indexes, as well as the amount of indexing necessary for each periodical, varies considerably. One periodical may require 3,300 entries to index annually and at the same time not have more than 40 subscribers on the total subscription list for the index in which it appears. Another magazine may be extremely popular and yet require only a few entries to index.

A charge is, therefore, fixed for each individual periodical indexed, based on two factors: (1) the number of entries required per year for the indexing, and (2) the number of subscribers to the index who subscribe to that periodical.

A basic rate per entry is established for each of the indexes by dividing the annual cost of the index by the total number of entries for the year. The basic rate is then, in the case of each periodical, multiplied by the number of entries required per year to index that periodical; and the multiple is divided by the number of subscribers there are to support the indexing of the periodical.

The result is the charge which each subscriber receiving the periodical must pay for its indexing for the year. The total annual subscription rate for each library is the sum of the rates for the indexing of all periodicals received by the library. By this method, the subscribers to each periodical are the ones to support the indexing of it. There is, however, a minimum charge for each index to insure that every subscriber makes his proper contribution towards total production costs.

Book Indexes

The scale of prices for Bibliographic Index, Book Review Digest, Cumulative Book Index, and Library Literature is likewise based on the amount of service rendered by the publication, and the amount spent annually for books has been chosen as the best measure of this service. Librarians are asked at intervals to report their annual book budgets and the libraries are arranged in a number of classes according to expenditures. Each library is then charged the rate for the class in which it belongs.

What to Report

After consultation with the Committee on Indexing Service of the Association of Research Libraries, it has been decided that in the interest of fairness and uniformity:

1. librarians should report the amount spent for books;
2. these figures should be reported for the three years previous to date of report;
3. charges for book indexes should be based on the average of book fund figures for the three years reported;
4. charges so established should remain in effect for a period of three to six years, after which a new report will be sought.

Appendix 3
Statement on the Library Licence Agreement
by the Booksellers Association[1]

'Many inquiries are received from members concerning the provisions of the Library Licence Agreement, and details are given below:

'The discount on net books which are governed by the Agreement may be up to 10%. In practice the maximum is expected by the library authorities, but booksellers should note that where trade terms on a particular book are less than $16\frac{2}{3}$% plus 5% (i.e. 20·89%) the Agreement provides for the full net price to be charged. It should also be noted that the library receives its preferential treatment in consideration, *inter alia*, of prompt and regular payment of its accounts. If the library does not keep to its own part of the bargain, the bookseller should notify his Association, who, as party to the Agreement, will refer the matter, where justified, to the Publishers Association.

'If a bookseller wishes to supply a library with net books at a discount, he should first of all approach the librarian and ask for his name to be added to the library's licence. The librarian, if he agrees, will then apply to the Publishers Association for the necessary endorsement. A bookseller should satisfy himself that he is authorized to supply at a discount by confirming with the librarian that the endorsement has been made on the licence.

'The grant of licences to the libraries is administered by the Publishers Association, working with the advice of an advisory committee on which the Booksellers Association is represented. Although the agreement applies mainly to public libraries, the conditions refer to libraries which "grant public access", and in

1. Quoted by kind permission of the Secretary of the Booksellers Association, from *Members' Bulletin*, August, 1963. It should be noted that the Library Association, formerly signatory to the Agreement, has withdrawn. Under a revised method licences are issued to booksellers, rather than to library authorities. That is, booksellers are authorized to supply the libraries entered on their licences with new books at the permitted discount. It is the bookseller who now applies for his licence to be endorsed with the names of the libraries he wishes to supply at a discount under the NBA. This reverses the method in operation up to 1963.

consequence, therefore, licences have in the past been granted to certain college and other institutional libraries which have satisfied the PA that their facilities are available for public use.

'A bookseller may, of course, supply any library with secondhand or non-net books, at any price he pleases, without such a licence. But where new net books are supplied by British publishers on the Standard Conditions of Sale of Net Books (as set out in the Net Book Agreement), *only a* licensed library may be given a discount, and then *only by booksellers whose names have been entered on that particular library's licence, by the Publishers Association.*

'Books imported from overseas publishers (whether direct or through a wholesaler) are not covered by the Library Licence Agreement, and the bookseller is not obliged to give the agreed discount on these. Care should be taken by the bookseller however to see if the publisher markets such books through an agent or associated company in this country with the power to maintain a published price and authorize a discount on it. In such cases, where the agent is a signatory of the Net Book Agreement, the library discount scheme would apply.'

Index